The one excuse and breath of art—charm."—*Stevenson.*

The Technique of Fiction Writing

By ROBERT SAUNDERS DOWST

TO

C. K. R. D.

Table of Contents

PREFACE

Many books have been written on fiction technique, and the chief excuse for the present addition to the number is the complexity of the subject. Its range is so wide, it calls for so many and so different capacities in one attempting to discuss it, that a new work has more than a chance to meet at least two or three deficiencies in all other treatments.

I believe that the chief deficiency in most works on fiction technique is that the author unconsciously has slipped from the viewpoint of a writer of a story to that of a reader. Now a reader without intention to try his own hand at the game is not playing fair in studying technique, and a book on technique has no business to entertain him. Accordingly, I have striven to keep to the viewpoint of one who seeks to learn how to write stories, and have made no attempt to analyze the work of masters of fiction for the sake of the analysis alone. Such analysis is interesting to make, and also interesting to read, but it is not directly profitable to the writer. It is indirectly profitable, of course, but it will give very little direct aid to one who has a definite story idea and wishes to be told the things he must consider in developing it and writing the story, or to one who wishes to be told roughly how he should go about the business of finding real stories. In fact, I believe that discussion and analysis of perfect work has a tendency to chill the enthusiasm of the beginning writer. What he chiefly needs is to be told the considerations he must hold in mind in conceiving, developing, and writing a story. The rest lies with his own abilities and capacities to work intelligently and to take pains.

Therefore the first part of this book takes up the problems of technique in the order in which they present themselves to the writer. Beginning with matters of conception, the discussion passes to matters of construction and development, and finally to matters of execution, or rather the writing of a story considered as a bare chain of events. Then the matters of description, dialogue, the portrayal of character, and the precipitation of atmosphere are discussed, and lastly the short story and novel, as distinct forms, are taken up.

PREFACE - 2

Usually the propositions necessary to be laid down require no demonstration; they are self-evident. That is why a book on technique for the writer need not indulge in fine-spun analysis of perfect work. Where analysis will lend point to the abstract statement, I have made it, but my constant aim has been not to depart from the viewpoint that the reader has in mind some idea of his own and wishes to be told how to handle it. Unquestionably literary dissection is useful in that it gives the beginning writer familiarity with the terminology and processes of the art, but the main object of a book on technique is to place the results of analysis, directly stated, in logical sequence.

I will note one other matter. A great part of the technique of fiction writing concerns matters of conception and development which are preliminary to actual writing. In fact they are essentially and peculiarly the technique of fiction. The story that is not a justly ordered whole, with each part in its due place and no part omitted, cannot have full effect, however great the strictly executive powers of its writer. Verbally faultless telling will not save a story which is not logically built up and developed, either before writing or in the process of writing. The art of telling a story is largely the art of justly manipulating its elements. The art of telling it with verbal perfection is not so much a part of the strict technique of fiction writing as it is of the general technique of writing. Therefore I have made little attempt to discuss the general art of using words. For assistance in studying the art of expression the reader should turn to a work on rhetoric. The subject is too inclusive for adequate treatment here. Moreover, it is debatable whether the art of verbal expression can be studied objectively with any great profit. But the art of putting a story together can be studied objectively with profit, and its principles are subject to direct statement.

I desire to acknowledge my indebtedness to Mr. William R. Kane, of The Editor Magazine, for much helpful criticism and many valuable suggestions.

INTRODUCTION

"A work of art is first cloudily conceived in the mind; during the period of gestation it stands more clearly forward from these swaddling mists, puts on expressive lineaments, and becomes at length that most faultless, but also, alas! that incommunicable product of the human mind, a perfected design. On the approach to execution all is changed. The artist must now step down, don his working clothes, and become the artisan. He now resolutely commits his airy conception, his delicate Ariel, to the touch of matter; he must decide, almost in a breath, the scale, the style, the spirit, and the particularity of execution of his whole design."

Thus Stevenson, in "A Note on Realism," takes it for granted that the artist in pigments, stone, or words cannot reproduce until he first has produced, cannot show a perfect work unless he paints, builds, or writes along the lines of a perfected design.

One cannot dabble long at architecture or the graphic arts without gaining keen realization of the fact that conception in its elaborative aspects is as much a part and phase of technique as the executive handling of materials. But the art of literature, and, more narrowly, the art of fiction, deal with materials other than those employed in the other arts; words, not colors or marble, nor yet sounds, are the resource of the story teller to precipitate his conception in enduring form; and words are at once frank and mysterious things. Their primary office is to forward the common business of life; each has some meaning in itself, more or less definite. It results that the writer of a story who sets out with only the merest glimmering of what he means to do in mind can produce a superficially plausible work, a work not too obviously misshapen, a work that means something, at any rate, although his failure to trace a design to guide his hand almost inevitably will prohibit his giving the basic conception most effective expression. And, since almost any sequence of words has some significance, it also results that the writer of fiction who works at haphazard may fail to discover that failure in his work as a whole is due to lack of planning rather than to defective execution. The mere grammatical coherence of a fictionally slipshod piece of work is a shield between its writer's inquiring eye and its essential defects.

The art of fiction is the art both of the tale and of the story, fictions that differ radically. Their most striking difference is stated in the following pages; here I can only remark broadly that the tale is episodal, consisting of a fortuitous series of incidents without essential connection or relation except that they all happened to happen to the characters, while the story is a whole in that each incident functions in the development of a plot or dramatic problem. If prevision and full elaboration of his basic idea are essential to the writer of a tale, they are doubly essential to the writer of a story, simply because a story is a whole and the result of careful co-ordination of parts. Even if the writer of some particular story has not worked along the lines of a fully elaborated design, the story actually will manifest co-ordination of parts or else be worthless. A story is more than a series of incidents; it is a series of incidents significant in relation to character. Its writer cannot set to work with an eye solely to the physical spectacle and follow after with his pen; he must prepare his people as well as the events, a task of cunning calculation. He must have an eye to many other matters, but this is not the place to state them. The matter of character is the matter significant here, because the whole difference between tale and story is made by the presence or absence of relation between events and personality. And it is certain that the writer of a story cannot hope to do the best work if he postpones until the moment of actual writing the task of moulding and elaborating his basic idea with a view to giving it maximum effect. The task to express perfectly, in a verbal sense, is difficult enough to claim the undivided attention of the ablest artist, but undivided attention cannot be given the matter of verbal expression by a writer who shapes his substance and picks his words at one and the same time. Either word or substance must suffer.

Accordingly, to emphasize the necessity that the writer of fiction give full shape and development to his design before writing, I have stated the necessity and discussed technique itself under two heads, conceptive or constructive technique and executive technique. To have carried this division rigorously through the whole book would have been neither possible nor profitable, for it would have involved much repetition and confusion, but the various items of technique are either largely conceptive and constructive or largely executive, and the best place to discuss each has not been difficult to determine. It was only necessary to contemplate the actual process of conceiving, developing, and writing a story, and to take up in their order the problems that confront a writer of fiction. The only matter which found no natural place, so approached, was that of characterization, which is almost equally a matter of construction and of execution, so that discussion of it has been broken up to some extent.

This approach to technique is the natural approach, and has been adopted for that reason. The more naturally and easily any study can be conducted, the greater the results that will be achieved. But there is a more immediate reason for taking up the phases of technique in the order in which they present themselves to a writer of fiction, thereby emphasizing the existence and importance of the constructive phases of technique. Briefly, it is that construction is at once easier and more important to learn than execution. Perhaps a little argument in support of the statement is called for.

It will not be questioned seriously that it is easier to learn the main principles of construction than it is to learn or discover how to write with finish and power. It is entirely possible to state abstractly the principles of construction, to grasp their reasons and implications from abstract statement, and to apply them by a mere act of the intelligence in writing any story. But it is entirely impossible to state abstractly the principles of writing with finish and power, or to learn to write so from any mere discussion of the matter. The condition is illustrated by almost any treatise on rhetoric, where half the text will be made up of examples transcribed to lend some weight to the obviously—and necessarily—inadequate discussion. How to write with finish and power can be learned only by long continued and intelligent practice, if it can be learned at all. Of course, this is not to say that constant practice is not necessary to gain any real facility and adequacy in applying the principles of construction.

The argument of the last paragraph is clinched by the fact that of a thousand stories, all of which are well constructed and put together, only a few or perhaps none will be written with any approach to real literary power, in the verbal sense. Of all the writers of to-day who can put together a story in workmanlike fashion how many have the power of the telling word? how many have even a style?

I have yet to substantiate the assertion that construction is more important for the writer of fiction to learn than execution, but the task is easy. In the last analysis, the power of a story, that is, its power to interest, depends upon its matter, the spectacle it presents. If the whole conception is justly elaborated and properly put together, it will have very nearly full effect, even though its writer does not give it perfect verbal expression, provided the verbal precipitation of the thing is not too shamelessly inadequate. Perfect verbal expression is necessary to give a properly constructed story maximum effect; it is not necessary to give it approximate effect. But perfect verbal expression will not save a story that is misshapen and distorted through lack of proper construction.

These considerations strongly urge the writer of fiction to master the principles of constructing a story before he frets about the nuances of expression, and just as strongly they impose upon a book on technique the obligation to discuss matters of construction at length and also to discuss them as such. The book which does not explicitly insist that certain matters are matters of construction, therefore to be performed before writing, is very apt to mislead. It is a defect from which too many books on fiction technique are not free, and one that I have tried to avoid.

How comprehensive and inclusive are the principles of construction the first half of this book attempts to show. Here it is enough to state that they embrace matters so different as the manipulation of possible incidents in the interest of climax, and the preparation or building up of the people of a story that its situations may have real dramatic value for a reader. The writer of fiction who merely writes cannot hope to provide by any instinct for these and the other matters of construction, and no power in his words can fortify essential weakness in his matter. Style, literary power, the right word in the right place—all will resist the tooth of time, but no one will preserve a story from the contagion of decay at the heart. Indeed, in the juster sense, a shapely design is the necessary foundation or basis for perfect writing, which is no mere varnish.

In this present era of magazine literature the chances are that nine out of ten actual or prospective writers of fiction who take up a book on technique for serious study will do so with an eye to the short story. And since this book is for the practitioner of the art, not for the mere reader of fiction, I have felt myself under obligation to discuss the short story and its peculiar technique with some approach to adequacy. Statement of the way the short story has been approached may serve to align the reader's mind with the argument.

In the first place, the short story is yet a story, a fiction, so that the general technique of fiction is applicable to it, with suitable modifications here and there. In the second place, the short story is a distinct type of fiction in that it embodies a plot or dramatic problem and is brief enough to read at one not very prolonged sitting. It is at once slighter and more pointed or direct than the long story of plot, the novel or romance. The result is that all its processes, particularly the process of characterization, must be conducted in a fashion more swift and summary than in a long story, and the difference is the whole of the difference in the technique of the two forms.

Unfortunately, a discussion of the peculiar technique of the short story cannot confine itself to this difference without failing to clear away the many misconceptions that becloud the subject. A good deal has been written on the short story, and, since there is really not very much to say, a good many writers have been led into nonsense. With so much misconception in the air, I have felt that it would be useful to state a tenable theory of the short story, and have attempted to do so in the chapter on the form. The matter will be found there and cannot be reproduced here, but brief statement of the argument will complete the foretaste of the book.

Since the short story is a story, at least, it may be divided and classified, like all stories, into stories of character, stories of complication of incident, and stories of atmosphere, that is, into stories which emphasize or stress the element of personality, the element of incident, or the element of setting. But the truly significant division of the short story into types, the division which it will be most directly profitable for the writer of fiction to realize, is twofold, not triplicate, and is the division into the dramatic short story and the short story of atmosphere or unity of emotional effect on a reader.

These two types are as different as black and white, and the misconception noted above consists in confusing them. The short story of atmosphere is Poe's sort of story; he said something definite and true about his peculiar art; but later writers, critics rather, have padded and distorted his words to cover the whole field of the short story. The general result is much printed folly, and the specific result for the short story writer is that he is continually urged, commanded, entreated, and advised to invest his work with some mysterious "unity." The advice is sound if the short story of atmosphere, the short story of unity or totality of emotional effect, is meant; the short story of atmosphere is a mysterious and subtle unity in that its people and happenings are curiously of a piece with its setting, serving to deepen or intensify the emotional effect of the setting on a reader. But, applied to the dramatic short story, the advice is unsound, for the dramatic short story may and usually does involve much diversity and contrast in its three elements of people, events, and setting. The only sense in which it can be said to be a unity is that it is verbally coherent, a single story. The single story may involve radically different people, happenings, and scenes.

The positive evil tendency in telling the short story writer to seek to invest his work with "unity" is that if he follows the advice his material will be restricted, and he will write stories too simple really to interest, apart from the appeal of their characters. And this point of interest brings up another aspect of this book which I would mention.

The last chapter states a general theory or philosophy of fiction which it will prove most profitable for the writer of fiction to grasp, however imperfectly I may have stated it. The theory is not profound, in the sense that it is mysterious, being merely the theory which is implied in the content and aim of the art of fiction itself. The content of fiction is man and what he may possibly or even conceivably experience; the aim of fiction is to interest, in Stevenson's words, "the one excuse and breath of art —charm." How much is implied in the content and aim of fiction I have tried to show in my closing pages, but the theory there stated is the guiding principle of the whole book, and any value it may have derives from such unforced handling of the subject. Apart from the merit of my own work, one thing at least is certain. If commentators on the art of fiction generally would deal less in "isms" and seek less to display their profundity and critical acumen, the actual writer of fiction might read them with some profit. As it is, the greatest single danger threatening the practitioner of the art is that his eagerness for all that pertains even remotely to his trade may lead him to take seriously the empty thunders of the schools and to forget that his business is to interest and captivate Mr. and Mrs. Smith, simply that.

To sum up, my desire has been to write a book that would be of some practical use, at least practically suggestive to the writer of fiction; therefore the only natural way to approach technique has been adopted, and I have indulged in analysis only when the analysis would be useful in itself or would serve to clear away misconception. In other words, the book has been written strictly for the writer, not the reader of fiction, and that implies much.

CHAPTER I - THE WRITER HIMSELF

Critical Faculty—Cultivation of Genius—Observation and Information—Open-mindedness—Attitude Toward Life—Prejudice and Provincialism—The Social Question—Reading—Imagination.

Accessible as are the data of the fiction writer, the facts and possibilities of life, their very accessibility places him under strict necessity to sift the useful from the useless in search for the pregnant theme. For if life presents a multiplicity of events to the writer, from which he may select some sort of story with little labor to himself, life also presents the same multiplicity of events to the reader, who can see the obvious as well as the lazy writer, and who will not be pleased with a narration of which he has the beginning, middle, and end by heart. A tale which does not interest fails essentially, and novelty, in the undebased sense of the word, is the root of interest. Therefore the writer of fiction who takes himself and his art seriously must develop the open and penetrating eye and the faculty of just selection. All is not gold that glitters, a fact that too often becomes painfully evident only when some tale discovered with joy and developed with eagerness lies coldly spread upon paper. The beginner who will approach his own conceptions in a spirit of unbiased criticism and estimation before determining to set them down will save himself useless labor, much postage, and many secret tears. Half of the essentially feeble work produced that has not a chance of getting published is the result of the writer's falling in love with his own idea simply because it is his own idea. The defect is in conception rather than in execution, and a matter of first importance to the writer is to develop the faculty of estimating his unelaborated ideas.

Unquestionably this faculty can be developed. The struggle for its development is half over, in a practical sense, when the writer comes to judge his concepts at all before writing, when he wins free of the habit of writing just to be writing, and of choosing to work on a particular tale because it is the best he can squeeze from his brains at the particular moment, rather than because it is absolutely good and he knows it to be absolutely good.

Unquestionably, too, the critical faculty is powerless to supply worthy conceptions. But that is beside the point. If the conceptions are worthy, the just critical faculty will recognize their merit, and give the writer courage and confidence to send each tale across the almost inevitable sea of rejections until it comes to port, as it surely will, if well done. And if the conceptions are feeble, and the writer cannot better them, it will be better for him and all concerned that he discover the truth.

Whether the essential genius of the teller of tales, the power that first supplies a theme of moment and then a fitting garb for it, is a plant capable of nurture, is not for me to attempt to show, or even to state. Fortunately, the question is academic. The dons may debate the point, but for those who themselves labor in the literary vineyard the thing to remember is that the same habits of observation and practice which some claim will create the literary faculty will at least foster its growth, if it is a gift, as others claim, and not to be artificially cultivated. Steady hours at the desk and moments with the notebook, the cultivation of the seeing eye, the informed mind, and the sympathetic heart, may not be able to create the divine spark. But it may burn within one for all that; and shall one neglect to bring it to full flame on the mere chance that it may not exist because of the possibility that it cannot be created? If the chance of its existence is great enough in the individual's eyes to justify the labor of writing at all, it is great enough to justify undertaking the correlative activities of observation and self-culture. At the least of it, these can result only in making one a better and more complete man or woman, irrespective of the literary result. The writer who fancies that his labor is but to string words, and that idea or passion come to life in the barren mind or heart, is foredoomed to failure. No equation can be formed between something and nothing, nor can something come from nothing. All life and all art is a quid pro quo; the writer must barter his time and sweat for his raw materials, ideas.

There is little need to state that of writers of equal genius the one with the deepest reservoirs of observation and information to draw upon will produce the more significant work. In relation to expository and argumentive writing the fact is patent; in relation to the writing of fiction it may be less obvious, but, curiously enough, is even more impressive when perceived. The writer of special treatise or argument may "devil" his subject for the occasion; though the writer of fiction may specially investigate the phase of life or society with which he deals, his investigations will aid him only in the external matters of dress, customs, speech, or atmosphere. For the preservation of the essential congruity and justness of the whole as a presentation of life he must depend solely upon his own innate familiarity with life, which cannot be brushed up for the occasion, for it necessarily derives from the totality of the individual's experience and the use he has made of it.

In this connection it may be noted that above all else the writer of fiction must be catholic in his interests and sympathies. He is the sieve through which the motley stream of life is poured to have selected for presentation its most significant aspects, and any unwisely cherished aversions of his are so many gaps in the netting through which, to his own loss, worthy matter constantly will escape. It is difficult enough at best for even the most open-minded writer to achieve some approach to an adequate presentation of a phase of life, and for the writer whose vision is distorted by prejudice and predilection, however perfect his technique, it is nearly impossible. The writer of fiction is concerned with political, social, or religious dogmas only in so far as they impinge upon and affect the individual life whose course his pen is tracing, and his only proper and fruitful attitude toward such dogmas is that of observer, not of fierce advocate or equally fierce assailant. The heart of the people is sounder than its head, perhaps because larger, and life is a complex of passion rather than a complex of intellectual crusades. The writer of fiction addresses the whole man, his emotional nature as well as his intelligence, and should address him by presenting the whole man, instead of some feeble counterfeit not actuated primarily by passion.

Emotion can be evoked only by the portrayal of passion, and emotion—sympathy, disgust, admiration, any spiritual excitement—is the root of the appeal of fiction. There are other elements of interest, primarily intellectual, as in the detective story or any story of ratiocination, but emotional appeal is the one essential in work of any compass. Emotional appeal is attainable only through a just presentment of life, and toward life the writer of fiction must preserve an attitude of observation and ready acceptance. In the last analysis, that is his business. The world pays its wage to the scientist for the narrow, intensive view; it pays its wage to the teller of tales for the broad, extensive view.

The course of letters is marked by great failures whose essential technical powers were nullified or at least hampered by their narrow outlook on life, and by great successes whose achievements bear the scar of prejudice and provincialism. In our day, the multitudinous standing controversies of the past have been reduced in bitterness by the more general diffusion of information and by the conflicting claims of more numerous interests that demand exercise. Nevertheless we still have the division between rich and poor, capital and labor, conservative and radical. For reasons immaterial here, this division and resulting social conflict will become more complete and bitter; the writer of fiction will face the fact and be forced to deal with it at times; and it is to be remembered that one may be abreast or even ahead of the best thought of the day without being hectic, and that to draw the conservative of fiction as a fool or a villain simply because he is a conservative is bad art. Conceivably a man may be back in the ruck of thought and belief because he is a fool, but he is not a fool merely because he is behind the times. He may have had no chance to learn better, and that is precisely the story.

Besides viewing life with a sympathetic and inclusive eye, the writer of fiction should investigate the smaller world of books. Life is infinitely more rich in substance than the printed word, but the observer is not a disembodied spirit, and cannot scrutinize the whole world, cannot exhaust even his own little neighborhood. He can call to his service the eyes of his contemporaries and of those who have gone before, and, in a few hours reading, can live vicariously a dozen lives. In this very real sense the world of books is practically larger than the actual world; one can hope to exhaust its more significant matter. By reading, the writer of fiction can gain familiarity with the actual tissue of life, the casual relation between motives and acts—so often obscured in real life—can mingle with nobler, baser, more significant people than he will be apt to meet, and can estimate the efforts of others in his own art. Reading of all sorts will yield information, and reading of fiction will reveal the root causes of success and failure in the difficult task to precipitate life in words.

There is little need to emphasize the difficulty of the task, twofold as it is. One must find matter, and one must display it. Not only will reading conduce to mental development and flexibility; it will reveal the function of the single word. Life is seen in chiaroscuro, but words are sharp and definite things. As Stevenson has said, the writer must work in mosaic, with finite and quite rigid words. If he really works, scorning to abuse a noble instrument and to prostitute a noble profession, his difficulties will but increase with his earnestness. Flaubert is a case in point. Only by reading can the writer discover the resources of language, and only by reading can he find encouragement in the spectacle of what patience and devotion have achieved.

One may employ a method of literary presentment diametrically opposite to that of fitting the right word in the right place, the method of taking a broad canvas, disregarding length, and, in a sort, modeling the verbal mass, which will possess plasticity to an extent, though composed of words intractable and rigid in themselves, like the atoms which compose modeler's clay. But this method is open only to the writer of a novel of epic length; the verbal economy of the short story forbids it; and it will usually be found that the books which manifest it—"Les Miserables," "David Copperfield," "Tom Jones," "Jean Christophe," "War and Peace," much of Thackeray's work, for instance—owe their appeal to the essential vitality and worth of their matter rather than to any detailed perfection of artistry. If the story is worthy, it will not be injured by compact and artistic expression; the function of the artist is to select the significant from life and to present it as pungently and as perfectly as possible; brevity in expression is as essential as economy of line in drawing. I have read and heard it stated that Stevenson and many others eminent for artistry are thin and self-conscious in their work, and personally I would give much to know whether this impression does not derive from the fact that many of the accepted great books of the world, and most of those appearing day by day, are negligible as examples of executive artistry, by their contrast making the occasional work that is concisely and artistically done seem somewhat artificial. The reader is perhaps so accustomed to imperfect work that the perfect has a touch of artificial glitter, and seems unreal. But this is a digression. The fact remains that the writer of fiction who would live by his art cannot afford to go in ignorance of what has been done before him. He should read, widely and with all his faculties on the stretch. A vast amount of experiment lies ready on the printed page. One may not by reading learn how to do perfect work, but one can at least discover what cannot by any possibility be done.

The general proposition is that the writer of fiction must observe life, must estimate it, and must express the phase that his estimation shows to be significant. The open eye, the cultivated and able mind, and the trained hand are all equally essential, and all must work together in harmony. Some have the eye without the hand; some the hand without the eye; in others the faculty of discrimination is wanting; but eye, mind, and hand may all be trained by application. No one who has not done his best has the right to complain of failure, and he who engages in the difficult business of letters, and neglects to use all efforts to equip himself, is a fool and nothing else. The writer may live in prosaic surroundings and be repressed by daily contact with people as dull as ditchwater; yet the world is wide and man a free agent within limits; let him strike his tent and go elsewhere. But let him first make quite sure that the defect is in his environment and not in himself. Otherwise, when ensconced in a snug artistic Bohemia, he may suffer the pain of learning that some quiet, clear-eyed seer has found rich ores in the old home life, and has wrought them to fresh shapes of beauty. And beyond the influence of all accidents of time and place lies the world of imagination, instinct with austere beauty, offering escape, solace, and rich gifts to him who has the golden key. Investigate the life that was Hawthorne's in Salem, Massachusetts, in the thirties and forties, then read "The Scarlet Letter," and turn your eyes within if ugliness lies stark about you. No boor and dullard may walk with you in the fields of fancy, alone with the night wind and the quiet stars. Dream with sanity, live with sanity, work with sanity and purpose, and realize that life and thought are your business, and that the stream of life as a whole is clean and fresh and sweet and utterly interesting even if you yourself are caught in some stagnant backwater. Open your eyes and swim for the clear reaches of the stream.

CHAPTER II - THE CHOICE OF MATTER

Selection—Sincerity—Adventure—Common Problems of Life—Originality—Novelty and Worth—Three Elements of Fictional Literature—Interest—Elements of Interest.

Life is infinitely various, and the possibilities of the imagination are even more extensive; the writer of fiction has enough material at hand. His primary task, to pitch upon a theme, is almost wholly selective, unless he is cursed with a paucity of observation or barrenness of imagination, in which case he has mistaken his calling. And in this task of selection the writer must bear in mind several considerations, his own predilections, his own powers, the intrinsic worth of the idea, and—last but not least—the audience he is to address. The writer should give ear to his own personal likings because he will do better work when he has interest in the matter under his hands; he should consider his own powers lest he attempt too much; he must consider the intrinsic worth of his theme lest his work be essentially feeble; and he must ponder his audience that his work may not go for naught. As to this last, a word of advice may not be out of place. Though the average reader may have little power to express, he usually has a well developed power to appreciate, and there is no need to "write down" to him. Condescension on the part of the writer of fiction is less obtrusive than in more directly informative writing, but it is instantly perceived and resented when present. The best audience for the writer to imagine is simply the best audience, alive in sensibilities and intelligence.

Stories—and therefore potential stories—may be divided roughly into two classes, those meant frankly to entertain and those designed to perform a higher function in addition. The line between them is not hard and fast; the same basic idea will slip from one side to the other under different handling by different authors. But there is a real difference, and that difference is made by the presence or absence of sincerity in the writer. The complete and rounded story will interest, which is the element of bare matter, will be so perfectly told that its mere structure will give pleasure, which is the element of artistry, and will truly express some phase of life as the author sees it, which is the element of sincerity. Stories may possess all, some, or none of these elements, but no story which does not possess them all can be said to fulfil completely the ideals of the art of fiction. There is no abstract obligation to be sincere resting on a writer of fiction; he should be sincere because his work will gain in power. A reader will feel the presence or lack of the quality.

This does not mean that the writer of fiction should take himself and life too seriously, a fault of which George Eliot is perhaps an example. He should simply be true to his own artistic convictions. If he must write "pot-boilers" for a living, he should refuse to let the hours so spent dull his artistic sense. No taint attaches to writing an entertaining story for the money in it; the elder Dumas, for instance, was a far greater artist in letters than hosts of more sombre writers who preceded and have succeeded him. And the writer who has Dumas' intrinsic gaiety and verve may write adventure and write literature too.

Back of the possibility lies the fact that the more bizarre phases of life are somewhat accidental and not very inclusive. The writer who deals with them must draw on his imagination heavily, not only for initial conceptions but for details. Very possibly he may miss some of the warm verisimilitude that derives from writing of familiar things and constitutes the keystone of the fictional arch. The strange and striking may gain a reader's superficial interest very easily, but "easy come, easy go" and the story of deep-rooted appeal is the story that displays to a reader sharply individualized human beings meeting the daily problems that are our common human lot. These problems are not dull because they are common and universal; their universality is the source of their interest. The writer who can reduce a general problem of love, hate, or labor to specific terms of persons and events, and can invest the whole with that certain momentousness, as of life raised to a higher power, which is the hallmark of literature, fulfils the highest possibilities of the art, whether he be as realistic in method as Dostoievsky in "Crime and Punishment" or as romantic in spirit as Hawthorne in "The Scarlet Letter."

Perhaps all this is somewhat repellent. We are not all Hawthornes in embryo—worse luck!—and though a good many aspire to do something worth while in itself some day, another good many are more humble, and incline to view the editor's check as sufficient warranty of success. Such an attitude is much healthier than that of the persecuted genius who refuses to investigate present conditions in the public taste and to coax and take advantage of them. But it may be carried to extremes. I do not think that many deliberately write trash, but it is apparent that a good deal of trash is written through too sedulous imitation of the tone of current literature. There is a recognizable type of machine-made story used by all the all-fiction magazines, and so forth. Subject to correction, I believe that the greater part of this cut-and-dried product is owing less to editorial conservatism than to authorial diffidence toward truly original work. Work may be original in substance, method, and viewpoint without being obscene or even "frank." When they do leave trodden ways, too many young writers persist in opposing the justifiable editorial reluctance to print anything that might give offense in a magazine of general circulation. The sex relation is not the whole of life, and even the sex relation may be treated, without the conventional sugar coating, to give all essential facts and make all essential comments and not be forbidding. We have a great world spread before us, and there is more in it for telling than is already printed and on the newsstands. When looking for a story, the thing to do is to forget those that have been written, to forget everything except the spectacle of life.

In the choice of matter the two main considerations are novelty and worth. Freshness in substance or form will go far to stimulate the writer and to sell the result of his labor, and essential worth is inspiring. No man finds pleasure in trivial and useless labor, but all normal men find pleasure and exhilaration in labor that is worth while. The writer who has worthy matter beneath his hands, and who knows it, will remain keyed to the requisite pitch during the labor of composition. Numbers have testified that the truest joy of authorship is found in conceiving and elaborating a tale before setting pen to paper, and time spent in estimating an idea and exhausting its possibilities and deficiencies before writing is necessary to make certain that the idea is worth while. Moreover, it is necessary that the writer know precisely what his idea is in order to develop it properly by excising the superfluous and emphasizing the significant. Conscious artistry is impossible unless the author knows definitely what he is striving to express.

The writer of fiction should bear in mind the three elements of the story that is literature, and should ask himself whether his projected tale is interesting, whether it is capable of being cast in literary form, and whether it is worth while. If the idea meets all these requirements, any failure in the completed work will be due to defective execution, not to deficiency in the conception. If the idea fails to meet the test as to form and worth, it may yet be worth while to write the story, for it may sell; if the idea is not interesting, it should be rejected without remorse. The first and highest function of a story is to interest and entertain; indeed, artistic form is but a means to that end, as is essential worth; and the dull, uninteresting story—a contradiction in terms—is the most woebegone literary failure under the stars.

The writer who allows any discussion of the art of fiction or the content of fiction to cloud for him the basic fact that fiction must be interesting is on the highroad to failure. It would be better for him had he never opened a book, except of frank adventure. Nine tenths of the ponderous and silly comment on fiction past and fiction present is written by critics and professors who first kick up a great dust over a work in order to display their insight in seeing through it, and nine tenths of that nine tenths—written purely from a reader's and not from a writer's standpoint— consists in appraising character by conventional ethical standards and in attributing to the writer whose work is under examination intentions and philosophies of which he never dreamed. It is at once very dull and very amusing, but the young writer whose eagerness for all information about his craft leads him to take such matter too seriously is in grave danger.

The writer of good fiction and the reader of good fiction are alike in that they both realize that the chief end of fiction is to entertain and interest, that perfection of form is desirable simply because it heightens the illusion of a story, and that worth of matter is necessary if the story is to be true literature because the cultured mind cannot find interest in the trivial. Culture has been finely defined as "the quality of a mind instinct with purpose, conscious of a tendency and direction in human affairs, able and industrious in distinguishing the great from the trivial." If this definition is valid—it bears its credentials on its face—great fiction may be defined as fiction which interests the cultured mind. The quality of arousing interest is the criterion and determinant, and implies perfection of form and essential worth of substance. The writer of fiction must never lose sight of the fact, nor of the resulting necessity that all his work be interesting. The fortunate thing is that fiction deals with so universal a thing as life; it need not repel the ignorant and uneducated in order to attract the abler mind.

The twin elements of fictional interest are the story and its people, and here becomes apparent the essential weakness of the story of mere incident. It cannot evoke interest as deep as that called forth by the story having closer relation to character. The range of character required by the story of incident is narrow; there are a thousand pregnant human qualities which the story of incident cannot first develop by action and then utilize to hold a reader's interest, but which the writer of the more leisurely and inclusive tale of everyday life can common can be truly vivified only by showing the person in acts displaying his essential traits, and the less dependence the action of a story has upon character, the less real to a reader will be the persons involved. The story of complication of incident, of mere structural ingenuity of plot, is superficially interesting, but it lacks the deeper appeal of the story which develops its people adequately. At any rate, it is true that a reader can love or hate characters, beside being interested in them; he can only be interested in an event. The people of a story are not to be neglected as sources of interest. They are harder to display than mere events, but they are infinitely more compelling. A bare series of events may interest, but the interest and appeal of what happens will be doubled if the observer is a friend of the persons affected, that is, if he knows them. The same is true in the case of a story. Its reader stands in the position of observer of events and people. The only trouble is that some stories have little action significant in relation to character, and when that is the case the writer loses one means to make his people real for a reader. The point to remember in searching for an interesting story is that the people are as influential an element as the events.

CHAPTER III - CONCEPTIVE TECHNIQUE: STORY TYPES

Conception and Execution—Utility to Know Types—Novel and Romance—Short Story—The Three Types—Emphasis—Three Elements of Any Story—Story of Character—Character and Action—Story of Incident—Archetypal Character—Short Story and Fallacy of Compression—Story of Atmosphere—Other Types.

The labors of the fiction writer are of two sorts, conceptive and executive. In actual practice, of course, the writer may have only the faintest glimmering of his story when he begins to write, and may simultaneously conceive, elaborate, and express as he goes along; but that is not the method of the conscious literary artist. An understanding adaptation of means to ends is impossible unless the writer has a definite purpose fixed in mind from the first moment of execution. And in writing on technique it is necessary to assume the natural order of the total artistic or creative process, whether the actual practice of any writer coincides with it or not. Therefore the body of conceptive technique first calls for treatment. Strict executive technique and also the technique of construction—which is both conceptive and executive—will be taken up after dealing with the matter of story types and the matter of plot.

I need not state that there is no technique of conception, mastery of which will yield the writer the golden secret of how to create or find a good story. That depends strictly on personal ability, and not on any objective knowledge of the mechanics of the art of fiction. But a knowledge of the several fundamental types of story, and of the how and why of the differences between them, cannot fail to aid the writer in estimating and realizing the potentialities and deficiencies of a particular idea. The writer who knows precisely where his story idea will classify under analysis has a standard that will prove most useful in the work of development. If it classifies as a story of atmosphere, rather than of plot or of character, the writer will be led to concentrate upon his proper task of creating the atmospheric illusion, and will not dissipate his energies and spoil the effect of the finished work by interpolating unnecessary touches of emphasis upon character or incident.

Another preliminary word may not be out of place. A story is a story, whether long or short; but the novel or lengthy romance is so much more inclusive in matter and complicated in structure than the short story—viewing the latter as a distinct literary type —that it is less essential for the writer of fiction of book length to know with exact definition the effect he wishes to produce than it is for the writer of the short story of a few thousand words. The potential and usual effects of the novel are many; it may and usually does contain chapters or passages emphasizing all three story elements of character, complication of incident, and atmosphere; but the short story is limited by its brevity to the creation of a single effect, and any touch of emphasis looking elsewhere usually will detract from the power of the whole. Therefore it is in short story writing that a firm preliminary grasp upon all the implications and connotations of the basic idea is most essential, also most attainable, and therefore a discussion of fundamental story types concerns itself largely with the short story. But much the same principles of constructive analysis utilized by the writer of the short story may be profitably employed in developing the various but more or less unified episodes of the novel.

The three fundamental types of story have a perfectly natural origin. A story is the relation of what (1) certain persons (2) did (3) in a certain place and under certain conditions of existence. Accordingly, as the elements of personality, action, or surrounding conditions are emphasized, we have the story of character, of incident, or of atmosphere. As Stevenson has said, there are but three ways to create a story, to conceive characters and select and devise incidents to develop them, to take a plot—a climactic series of incidents—and devise characters to enact it, or to take an atmosphere and precipitate it as best the writer may.

There is, however, an obvious fact to remember. These several types of story differ from one another only in point of emphasis; in each case an element possessed by all is stressed; no type is entirely devoid of the elements emphasized in the other two. An intended story lacking any one of the three elements of character, of complication of incident, or of setting is not a story, but something else. The most common example is the composition portraying character without any plot or complication of incident, which is not a character story, but a character sketch. It cannot be too strongly insisted that a story is a story, consisting of a climactic series of incidents, as distinguished from a tale, which is a level series of incidents, unrelated save in that all happen to the same group of characters. Plot is a matter not specifically under discussion as yet, but half the difficulty and most of the inutility in writing on fiction technique reside in the fact that one must treat in isolation matters which are but elements of a unified artistic synthesis. A story is a story; its people do not merely exist, they live and act. In the case of the story of complication of incident, the complication supplies the story-element of the fiction; in the case of character story, the evolution or degeneration of character supplies the story-element; while in the case of the story of atmosphere, the climactic progression of the particular emotional impression to the point of highest intensity in itself supplies much of the plot- or story-element of the conception.

Another qualification should be stated. The normal story, written for its own sake, is emphatic in that it stresses some one of its three elements. But there is also the thematic story, written to vivify an abstract proposition or to point a moral. The type lays no special emphasis on character, incident, or setting, and is written with an eye to an ulterior purpose beyond the mere sake of the story. It is not a natural type, and may be disregarded here. Incidentally, it is not a very successful type, and of course any success it may achieve as a work of art cannot derive from the truth or weight of the proposition or moral behind it.

Starting from the proposition that there are three normal story types, it may be profitable to examine them in detail. I am not yet concerned with the technical devices whereby character may be drawn, a plot devised and narrated, or atmosphere created; my sole purpose is to suggest how the writer may recognize the true character of his idea, that in developing it he may know exactly what he is trying to do.

The story of character is concerned with the infinitely diverse traits of our common human nature as manifested by the people of a story. The single trait or few traits, rather than the totality of each person's nature, should be sought to be developed, for reasons that a moment's thought will render apparent. Character can be truly realized only by showing the person in characteristic actions and, unless the writer desires to extend his work to a great length, he can formulate no course of action which will illustrate a complete personality. In all its aspects, fiction is a matter of selection, and the writer of a story of character should concentrate his powers of description and exposition upon the traits of personality involved in the acts of the persons. The short story must present a relatively incomplete picture of each character's soul; the novel may approach each person from a number of angles; but even the novelist should consider whether he cannot give maximum reality and vivacity to his people by not attempting a too complete presentation of each.

If, then, the initial conception of a story involves or suggests true traits of character, it may be advisable to develop the story so as to throw into strong relief the quality or qualities involved. The possibility of the wisdom of such development becomes a probability if the traits are somewhat novel and not those possessed in common by all men to some extent, such as the capacity to love, to hate, to sacrifice self, ambition, the fear of death, and so forth.

It should be remembered that the hallmark of the true character story is its progression; the persons of the story grow stronger or weaker in their respective traits under the pressure of events. There is a climactic moment of indecision and suspense when it is doubtful whether the character will shape circumstances or circumstances the character. This distinguishing attribute of the character story is its essential quality as a story; the strict type is debarred from recourse to complication of incident to save it from being a mere sketch; change or progression in the characters is itself the story or plot element of the fiction. Realization of the fact will give the writer a firmer grasp on the truth that characters and events must be developed in strict concert and harmony. Anticipating later statement a trifle, let me say that portrayal of the actions of a character is portrayal of the character himself, so that his actions must be characteristic, or two elements of the story will be at cross purposes. In setting out to write a character story, the author deliberately chooses to emphasize character and to depend for interest on the spectacle of its evolution or degeneration. Since he is after all writing a story—though of one type—the author must devise some climactic series of incidents. But the character element is the preponderant strain of the fiction, and each successive incident should be chosen with an eye to that element, and its climactic value should inhere in its being climactic and progressive in relation to the trait of character sought to be developed.

This is all somewhat abstract, but the test is much easier to apply to a concrete story idea than it is to formulate in terms. If the idea consists of a tentative grouping of incidents which suggests an interesting phase of character in an interesting phase of development, the conception may be elaborated into the story which emphasizes character. On the other hand, if the initial idea is simply of a phase of character which can be adequately shown in progression by a series of incidents devised to that end, the same treatment is advisable. In each case it is possible that such treatment will give maximum effect to the conception.

The story of complication of incident interests primarily because of its plot, and not because of its people or the totality of its emotional effect.[A] It is more than a type of story; in a way it is really the archetype of all stories. An historical analysis will show the truth of the statement. First came the tale, a chain of incidents having no essential connection except that they all happened to the characters. Then came the story, a chain of incidents which are not fortuitous and accidental, but each essential to the whole design. And from the story have sprung such variations as the character story, which emphasizes the element of personality, and the story of atmosphere, which emphasizes the setting, spiritual or material. But the story of plot, which stresses the bare incident, is archetypal of all fiction in that interest centers in the story rather than in the persons or their environment. Perhaps the French conte, or brief dramatic narrative, is the strictest story type of all.

I have chosen to touch upon the character story first, rather than the more fundamental and inclusive story of plot, simply because the potential story of plot is easily recognizable, and my sole aim here is to state some of the tests which the writer may apply to his idea after conception to discover its true character, that he may know how to handle it. The germ of a plot can be distinguished at a glance, while the question of what a plot really is requires separate treatment.

If the writer would produce a strict short story, he cannot rest content with the apparent fact that his initial conception is the germ of a story plot, that being the case. The story of plot may be easy to recognize as a genre, but not all stories of plot are potential short stories. All plot germs are not susceptible of adequate development within the narrow limits of the short story. Ten thousand words is probably the extreme limit of the type as a commercial possibility, and, in a space so brief, if the chain of events is at all complicated or lengthy, it is impossible to bring out all its nuances and implications. Too many critics and writers seem to entertain the idea that the short story is the result of compression, but emphatically that is not true. The synopsis of previous chapters before an instalment of a serial novel is an example of compression, and a most repellent one. A short story is the result of its own inherent brevity. A naturally long story, it is true, may be shortened materially by mere rhetorical compression, but it cannot be rendered a short story thereby, for the short story develops its fewer incidents with as much rhetorical elaboration as the novel or romance develops its many happenings. The short story that is a short story—such as Kipling's "Without Benefit of Clergy," Stevenson's "Markheim," or Poe's "Fall of the House of Usher"—gives off no impression of verbal bareness. The short story is a literary form, with all the elaboration of expression that the term implies. Its brevity results from careful selection of the incidents to be set forth, and not from concise expression of an indiscriminate welter of incidents.

Undoubtedly the matter requires emphasis. Too much has been written and said as to the necessity of compression in short story writing. If what is meant is rhetorical compression, bare statement without verbal elaboration, no such necessity exists.

What is necessary is care in making certain that the story is a short story, and care to relate nothing not essential to its development.

The French type of short story in general, and Maupassant's work in particular, are often cited to illustrate the need for compression. In the first place, the essential genius of the French language is such that in translations, to English or American apprehension, fully elaborated statement often seems somewhat bare. Moreover, I cannot admit that Maupassant's best work is equal in rounded artistry and appeal to that of others who have chosen to write less barely and mathematically. If compression means anything, it means squeezing something into less space than it would normally occupy, which is not artistry, but an attempt to do in execution the proper work of conception and construction, to devise a story which can be given adequate literary expression in a limited number of words.

A critical reading of almost any successful short story will disclose that the manner of its telling is as truly the source of its interest and appeal as is the novelty or human importance of the naked story idea. The difference between a recital of facts and a work of fiction is the difference between mere reporting and true literature. The writer who strives to compress in expression, instead of carefully selecting the matter for expression, deliberately rejects his only means to produce a sufficiently full and rounded presentment of the particular phase of life he seeks to depict. That means is to write with due elaboration, lest the phrasing seem stark and flat in comparison with the softly moulded contours of life itself. There are two elements in literature, the fact and the form; they are equally important and should be equally complete. When considering the fitness of a plot to serve as the skeleton for a short story, remember that in execution the thing must be written with due verbal elaboration, else it will be angular and unattractive, and that the idea of many incidents, people, or places cannot be so written in the space available. In execution, write adequately, and in conception and construction, select.

The story of atmosphere, which emphasizes the setting in which its people move, and seeks to bring out the emotional value of the physical or spiritual environment, is not difficult to recognize, being like the story of plot in this respect. But it is most difficult to do well. The story of character deals with concrete people, and the story of plot deals with concrete events; the story of atmosphere deals with these and something more, an intangible sensual or emotional impression, as of beauty or horror, correspondingly more difficult to create. It demands imaginative powers of the highest order, and perfect technical powers. Within limits, the unimaginative author may write effectively of characters and events, for he can see and study them objectively in daily life, and, again within limits, they may also be presented effectively by matter of fact phrasing. But atmosphere cannot be seen—even physical atmosphere must be felt, or there is no emotional effect—and all the resources of language at times become pitifully inadequate to precipitate an emotion. It is all a matter of clear conception and careful design, and the secret cannot be stated, but must be learned, each for himself. However, I am not concerned in this place with executive technique, or even with constructive technique, and whatever hints can be given as to the creation of atmosphere would be out of place. My object is merely to state the fundamental types of story and the necessity that the writer recognize the true character of his conception, that he may develop it with emphasis properly laid.

Other types of story exist, but the lines between them are not drawn by the inherent character of the art of fiction. The love story, for instance, may be told with emphasis on character, on incident, or on atmosphere, and the placing of emphasis determines its artistic character. The technique of conception is concerned only with fundamental types, and the sole object of its mastery is to give the writer knowledge of the essential artistic character of each of his conceptions, that he may work with a definite aim in development. My object is not to discuss or analyze pedantically, for the sake of the analysis itself, but simply to state the importance of discovering the basic fictional character of the idea, that it may be properly expanded. Strict constructive and executive technique of course require separate treatment.

CHAPTER IV - CONCEPTIVE TECHNIQUE: PLOT AND SITUATION

Definition of Plot—Character and Plot—Dramatic Value of Plot—Complication—Interest—Plot as Problem—Three Basic Themes—Conflict Between Man and Nature—Conflict Between Man and Man—Conflict Within the Same Man—Arrangement of Elements of Plot—Climax—Major Situations —Situation and Plot.

The plot of a story is its heart and essence. This is obviously true in the case of the strict story of plot, and it is very curiously true in the case of the story of character or of atmosphere. For in the story which lays emphasis on personality, the evolution or degeneration of the particular trait which has been selected for presentation is the real story-element of the fiction. The fact is the root of the necessity that the action develop in concert with the trait of character, giving it opportunity for expression. And in the story which lays emphasis on atmosphere, the climactic progression of the particular atmosphere to the point of highest intensity is the real story-element, which is the root of the necessity that the action develop in strict keeping with the atmosphere, that the effect may not be spoiled.

What is a plot? Many attempts at definition have been made, and the results have not been illuminating. Everyone has an idea of what a plot is, but those who have attempted to state their conception briefly have encountered difficulties. Perhaps an indirect approach to the problem will yield results.

A tale is not a story, for a tale is a relation of events which happened to happen to the characters. It is episodal, and the interest of the thing inheres in each episode separately, not in the whole. There is no essential connection between the incidents, except that they all happened to the same group of characters. The contrary is true of a story, interest in which is in the whole, as a progression, and, since the difference between tale and story is made by the presence or absence of plot, it appears that a distinguishing mark of a plot is that its events function together as a unit. There is some connection between them other than chance, and that connection lies in the intimate relation between the events of a story and its characters. Event and personality each influence or even determine each other simultaneously. Incidentally, realization of the fact will free the writer from any misconception that the action and the characters are separable elements of a story. For instance, jealousy, a trait of character, may cause a murder, an event, and a husband's chance opening of a letter addressed to his wife, an event, may give rise to Jealousy, the trait of character. Or the husband's loyalty will be strengthened in the fiction if he refuses to credit appearances.

Interaction, then, between incidents and characters, arising from the unity of the whole conception, is the first essential element of a plot. The second essential element—and there are but two—is that the several incidents of the story possess climactic value, not necessarily climactic value in the sense of ascending tensity—though that is most desirable—but climactic value in that each event should have influence in forwarding the story to a definite end, that state of quiescence which is not attainable in real life short of the grave, but which fiction must postulate. In other words, since a plot is made up of incidents which influence and are influenced by the characters, and since the story must move to an end, a plot presents a problem. What will the persons do? if the emphasis is on personality; and what will happen? if the emphasis is on the event.

To state it in the form of a definition, a plot is a series of events which influence and are influenced by traits of personality, and which are climactic in that they move to a definite conclusion, so that the series embodies some problem of life brought to solution.

I state this merely for what it may be worth, which possibly is no great matter to the writer of fiction. Plots are not to be found by vivifying a definition, but a definition may prove useful in testing a story idea when it is found, and the object of the whole discussion is merely to give the writer some aid in appraising the essential fictional value of his conceptions.

The fact that a plot is a problem gives the several events their climactic value. They are steps and approaches to the solution. And a plot is a problem simply because fiction concerns man, while man is a free agent, in possibility at least. Given certain characters and an event bearing upon them, and the problem of what they will do instantly arises, and the problem of the ultimate result of their actions. Given certain events, to reverse the emphasis, and characters on whom they bear, and the same problems arise. A plot is question and solution in one, and the solution must inevitably follow from the characters and events.

It will be perceived that the distinguishing quality of a plot is its dramatic value. A plot is a problem of life, and a problem is a conflict between opposing forces. Event and character wrestle with one another, and the outcome is doubtful, wherein lies the interest of the story. It is accurate to state that the conflict is between event and character, for though character may struggle with character, nevertheless the struggle is operative only in action, and the opposed persons struggle with the doings, not the naked souls, of each other.

It will be perceived also that the element of complication is not essential to a plot, as Poe has pointed out. Of course, in the story of incident, where the reader's interest centers chiefly in the events, not in the characters or atmosphere, complication is most useful, and in fact supplies much of the problem- or plot-element of the fiction. But complication is not a sine qua non, and should not be so regarded. Complication of incident, indeed, in the story which is fundamentally of character or atmosphere, may prove a positive handicap, adding to the difficulties of execution and spoiling the unity of effect, if the fiction is a short story. As has been stated, the novel is a broader canvas, without a single emphasis if the writer wills, and here, within the limits of naturalness, complication of plot is thoroughly desirable. Any bid for a reader's interest is of use, only in the short story the writer must necessarily limit himself to one sort of bid.

At that last of it, pretty nearly all of the technique of fiction writing has root in the necessity first to gain the reader's interest and then to hold it. That is the real object of perfection of form, even, and the device of plot has root in the same object. In simpler and more unsophisticated ages the stage presented not drama but mere spectacles, as the tale did in the spoken word or printed page; the plot, lending to the play its dramatic character and to the fiction its story character, developed only when audience and readers lost the child's vivid interest in whatever he sees, and began to yawn at the episodal. Pageantry and the unrelated event became stale, in comparison with the spectacle of life itself, and then plot was found, a method of isolating a single one of life's strands, and, by showing it in high relief, lending it an added dignity and appeal.

The basis of the more intense appeal of the plot over that of the episode is psychological. The hardest thing in the world to do is to make a reader think, but the reader who does think is interested. That is why he is thinking. Since a plot is a problem, the reader of a story of plot is made to think, and the matter impinges upon him with some force. To repeat former phraseology, if the emphasis is on the events, he tries to figure out what will happen, at least wonders about it; if the emphasis is on the characters, he tries to foresee what they will do. Incidentally, the reader of to-day is habituated to the story of plot. If nothing happens he will chalk a black mark against author and magazine, as the editor knows.

As has been said—and emphasis is not out of place—a plot is a problem. Problem, in this connection, means conflict between opposing forces, which gives the various events and situations of a story any dramatic value they may possess. It follows that there are three basic plot-themes, conflict between man and his environment or Nature, conflict between man and man, and conflict between opposed traits in the same man. It will be profitable for the writer to bear this in mind when combing the world for his story.

In his essay on Victor Hugo's romances, Stevenson has touched upon the emergence in fiction of the conflict between man and Nature. Briefly, his argument is that in the works of such a one as Scott the world and natural forces serve but as stage and stage devices for man and his doings, while Hugo, particularly in "The Toilers of the Sea," draws storm, cold, and heat as man's active enemies, almost endowing Nature with a vindictive personality. Whatever the fact as to Hugo, it is certain that to those who meet her face to face on sea and land Nature is a somewhat stony-hearted mother, yielding food and shelter only at the pistol-point of toil and struggle. To those of us who live in cities, and whose concerns are mainly social, the constant struggle of mankind against drought and flood, storm and cold, fire and famine is obscured, but it is a living reality, nevertheless, and a rich source of fiction that will get under the skin of the most pampered apartment-dweller. The roots of our lives stretch far into the dim past, when the unending struggle with natural forces was a bitter reality to all, and adequate fictional presentment of the struggle with Nature often proves to have an incisive appeal wanting in less fundamental themes. Particularly, the writer may rely upon such a story's appealing to the cultured and the uncultured mind alike, for the intrinsic human importance of its theme is felt by all. The elements of the dramatic problem presented are so simple that previous familiarity with them in personal experience is not essential to their understanding.

A fine example of this theme given short story treatment is Bret Harte's "The Outcasts of Poker Flat," while the portions of Stevenson's "Kidnapped" dealing with David's experience on the Isle of Earraid and his flight through the heather with Alan Breck find their dramatic quality largely in the same theme. It is interesting to note that Harte, however, does not emphasize the conflict between man and Nature to the utmost of possibility, for in his story there is much emphasis on character and the struggle of man with man. Whether the story gains or loses in total effect thereby is immaterial; it will prove an interesting experience for the writer to recast the tale so as to bring out more exclusively the theme of conflict with Nature. In connection with the general discussion as to plot, I will state that if Harte had entirely excised the theft of the party's horses by the treacherous member, and had not brought out the contrast between the gambler, the prostitutes, and the innocents, the story still would have been adequately plotted. The bare situation of men and women snowbound in a mountain cabin is a plot germ, for it suggests the problem whether they will survive or perish.

The plot which presents conflict between man and man is distinctly social in nature. The possibilities for the writer of fiction in the general scramble for the almighty dollar, the rivalry of love, the desire for revenge, and a thousand other passions and ambitions that bring man into conflict with his fellows, are practically infinite. Three minutes spent in running over this field for plots will demonstrate the folly of bewailing the lack of something fresh to write about. Perhaps some ingenious mathematician, given the data that there are a hundred million men and women in the United States, and that each one has some small number of desires and passions active or dormant, will calculate the potential conflicts resulting. Each conflict is the seed of a plot, and each plot may be written a hundred times, each story being made different from the last by varying the manner of treatment. There is not too little to write about; there is so very much that keen selection is essential.

Any magazine offers examples of the exploitation, by short story writers, of the conflict between man and man, while to portray the conflict is peculiarly the field of the novel, with its social emphasis. Balzac and Thackeray are supreme masters in presenting a slice of the social spectacle; "Vanity Fair" and "Cousin Pons" depict struggle between their people, and but little else. At the top of the social ladder the struggle is carried on by intrigue and sugared words, at the bottom with the knife and naked fist, but the struggle is the same in essence, and of enthralling interest to a reader. All the world loves a winner, and all the world wants to find out whom it is to love. The mere mechanical details wherein the struggle finds expression and operation are the least of the plot, which is indebted for its dramatic quality to the bare fact of struggle. Doubtless the girl who runs daily to the public library for a novel would be shocked to be told that she is impelled by the same human quality that makes street-loafers and passersby gather about two fighting boys, but she is, nevertheless. The writer who would please her—and her father, mother, and brothers—will do well to remember the fact.

The story which seeks to present conflict between two opposed traits in the same man or woman is most difficult to write so as to create any fictional illusion. It deals almost exclusively with psychological data, of the facts of the soul, and requires knowledge and imaginative insight as well as verbal dexterity. It is supremely easy to conceive a plot involving struggle of the man with himself, but it is supremely hard to give such a struggle objectivity, to expand it into a fiction operative in action and yet developing the internal conflict. I cannot think of a finer example than Stevenson's "Markheim." A close and critical study of this story by one who is qualified to taste its full flavor will reveal at once the great difficulties that face the writer who chooses such a theme, and the high pitch of achievement attainable through proper handling of material.

The greatest practical drawback to the giving of much time to mastering the technique of soul-analysis lies in the narrow appeal of such a story even when perfectly conceived and written. To recur to the always apposite Stevenson, it is safe to say that his "Dr. Jekyll and Mr. Hyde" is a thousand times more interesting to the average reader than "Markheim," simply because the soul-struggle is so much more completely made objective and given expression in action in the first fiction than in the second. This is done so very emphatically that nine readers out of ten entirely miss the point of "Jekyll and Hyde," and fail to realize that the struggle is between two tendencies in the same man, who is split into his good and bad selves merely for the sake of concreteness. Most fiction readers have little love for abstractions and fine spun analysis—witness the common repute of Henry James, to an extent undeserved, it may be said in passing. Exclusive emphasis upon the struggle of the man with himself will tend to confine the writer's appeal to the intellectuals, in the special modern sense, a matter inimical to the pocketbook, at the least of it. Psychological analysis is most useful in developing almost any type of story, but as the sole theme for a fiction it has its disadvantages.

When the writer has his hands on a plot, of whatever type and however found, his conceptive labors are by no means over. It remains to recast and rearrange the elements of the idea, that the most effective arrangement may be discovered. A first invention is very rarely incapable of improvement, and in the interests of artistry the author should exhaust all the possibilities of his idea before writing, that he may not chance upon unsuspected potentialities in his story only when it is half written, or not discover them at all. Within limits, of course, any story will tend to shape itself; in particular, there is much testimony as to the intractability of characters; but one cannot consciously strive to do any particular thing or to produce any particular effect without first knowing just what the thing or effect is to be.

Possibly the most important matter is to arrange the incidents, the separate elements of the problem or conflict which the plot presents, in such manner as to give the progression a climactic character. Not only should each major event be a definite step toward the conclusion, solution, or denouement, but each succeeding event should be more striking, significant, and tense than its predecessor. This sort of climactic movement is not essential to a plot, but it is an essential element of a good plot, particularly a good plot for a short story. The short story is a much more strict and artificial type of fiction than the novel; in other words, its writer has fewer resources to impress a reader, and he must utilize to the full whatever is open to him. Among his resources is the device of sensible movement to a crisis or climax. Like the rest of fiction technique, the device is useful because it tends to keep alive and stimulate a reader's interest. This it does because ascending tensity suggests further struggle. Any flat incident, on the contrary, less tense or striking than its predecessor, infallibly suggests that the story is already falling to its end, and the end seems dull because the problem is not fully worked out or even stated. Psychologically, the point is delicate; it is a queer paradox that a reader at once hates to think and yet wants to be made to think. But that is a reader's condition. With equal readiness he will welcome climactic movement and continue to read, or welcome any premature fall in tensity and throw the story aside.

To show by example the results that may be achieved by use of the device of movement to a climax is impracticable; these matters that cannot be displayed by pungent quotation the student must dig out for himself by intelligent reading. Almost any successful story will display climactic arrangement of its major events. I cannot forbear to mention the ascension whereby Thackeray leads a reader of "Vanity Fair" up to Rawdon Crawley's confrontation of Becky and Lord Steyne. Hawthorne's "The House of the Seven Gables," a book in most respects so totally dissimilar, shows a like process in leading up to the death of Judge Pyncheon. George Douglas's "The House With the Green Shutters," less widely known, is strongly climactic in its latter part. But examples, in short story and novel, are infinite in number and sort.

To recapitulate, a plot is a problem of human life brought to a fitting and convincing solution, and consists of a series of events which displays the fact and result of a conflict between opposing forces, spiritual and material, actuating and affecting men and women. Therefore the chief characteristic of a plot is its dramatic value. The definition may be turned to use not so much in the discovery of plots as in appraising their fictional value, their power to arouse and hold a reader's interest, after they have been found or invented.

Since a plot is a conflict between opposing forces, and since fiction deals with man, the three fundamental plot-themes are conflict between man and his environment, conflict between man and man, and conflict in the soul of the same man. Realization of the fact will serve to give point and definition to the writer's search for the idea.

Finally, a just regard for his readers will lead the writer to cast his incidents into some climactic arrangement. The first, last, and only proper aim of a story is to interest, and break in the expected movement to a climax is fatal to interest.

It would be interesting to go into the matter of plot-analysis at some length—I have in mind particularly the deficiencies of Poe's definition that a plot is a series of incidents contrived to produce a single effect—but this book is for the writer. I shall try throughout to keep to the writer's viewpoint and to develop nothing not of practical utility in the work of conception, elaboration, and execution.

Thus far the discussion has been concerned with plot as a whole; it remains to consider the events, incidents, or situations which compose a plot. The situations of the plot or story are what its writer must cast into a climactic consequence, and he must have some standard to measure each before he can determine its proper place.

The fictionally significant aspect of a plot is that it embodies a conflict between opposing forces, that is, it is dramatic. Likewise, the fictionally significant aspect of a situation is that it displays opposed persons—or at least opposed forces—in conflict. The writer manipulates his material—preferably before writing—so that two or more persons, actuated by incompatible motives, are brought into conflict; there is a moment of indecision; then some person bends the other or others to his will; and the situation determines. Or the writer brings a character or group of characters into conflict with Nature, as did Harte in "The Outcasts of Poker Flat." Here, also, there is a period of indecision, and then either the human force or the natural force triumphs.

The dramatic quality of any situation inheres in the struggle between opposing forces which each presents, and rises or falls with the essential strength of such forces. Take two instances of conflict between opposed motives in the same person. In some humorous story a character may be unable to decide which of two women he wants to marry. One can cook, let us say, and he is a gourmand; the other is pretty, and he has leanings that way, too. The dramatic quality in such a story will be slight, because the motives involved are relatively weak, yet it will be present. But take the story of a French girl who is outraged by a German soldier and gives birth to a child by him. Her quality of patriotism can be built up to great intensity, if the writer wills, even to the point where the reader will accept an impulse on her part to kill her child. Her quality as a mother can be built up likewise. It would be a most effective touch to have her hate the unborn child furiously, then to arrange matters so that she should be unable to carry out her first impulse to kill it and be forced to care for it, giving it opportunity to awaken her dormant maternal instinct. Finally, love for France and hatred for Germany can be stimulated again, so that she is shown veering between the impulse to kill and the impulse to cherish. Such a situation is intensely dramatic, for it involves conflict between two of the most intense human qualities, love of one's country and love of one's child. The more terrific the opposed forces in any situation, the higher its dramatic value.

At first glance it may seem that the relative position in a story of each of its various major situations is determined by the plot itself, but that is not the case. It appears to be the case because it is usual to regard the plot of a story as the entire mechanical arrangement of the fiction, including the nature and order of the situations, which is a false view of plot. As the previous discussion has attempted to demonstrate, plot is merely the conflict between opposed forces of personality and environment, at least one of the forces being of personality. Any two stories which display conflict between the same forces have the same plot, though one may vary widely from the other in the means employed to give the struggle objectivity and expression in action.

The writer of fiction should realize the point. The imagination produces concrete pictures and conceptions, and, when a story is imagined, it will come to life in terms of concrete people and events, more or less definitely ordered and determined. But the writer should not stop there. He should ascertain just what opposed forces of personality or environment give the story and its situations plot and dramatic value, and then should seek to find whether he cannot give the basic conflict involved more effective presentment than will be given by the persons and situations which he has already conceived. An essentially weak conception may offer a clue to a dramatic conflict that will have fictional power if properly developed by persons and situations different from those first conceived.

It will be perceived how far it is within the writer's power to manipulate situation in the interests of art, which, in this connection, means climax. Starting with some basic conflict, which will be his plot, the writer can devise situation after situation in which the struggle will become more and more acute, until, finally, it will become so serious as to involve all the elements of the story. And with the determination of the dramatic situation which involves all the elements of the story, the story itself will terminate, for the struggle which it embodies will have been settled one way or the other. This final situation will be the climax of the story, and its outcome or result will be the denouement. The story will be ended because the struggle or conflict it serves to embody will have ended. One force or the other will have triumphed.

In considering the question of situation, the writer of fiction is considering a more specific aspect of the question of plot. Usually he desires to find a plot of real dramatic value, and likewise he usually desires to find a situation or situations of real dramatic value. The dramatic value of plot and of situation resides in the struggle between the opposed forces which it presents. The more powerful the forces involved in either case, the greater the dramatic value of the conception. Each major situation of a story derives its dramatic quality from the opposition of incompatible motives or forces that endows the story's plot with its dramatic quality. In fact, it is not too loose to say that the situation of a story is its plot, provided the main situation or climax is meant.[B]

The purpose of the action or incidents of a story is to give the dramatic struggle it embodies concrete expression. That is to say, the dramatic quality of a story is specific in relation to certain persons and certain events. Two definite men, for instance, will engage in a definite fight over a definite woman. The writer will seek to individualize the persons involved, which is a matter of description and characterization, and he will seek also to picture the physical struggle as definitely as possible, which is a matter of descriptive narration. It is not enough to conceive a plot or dramatic situation; the writer must also expand it into a story, which should be as concrete and specific as its nature permits. Only thus can a reader be made to feel the essential power of the whole conception. It follows that the action or incidents of a story should be devised with a view to express the dynamic elements of the plot and that no incident should be incorporated in the story unless it will serve to build up some one of the forces involved or else serve to illustrate the conflict of forces that have been built up previously.

CHAPTER V - CONSTRUCTIVE TECHNIQUE
OF NARRATION

See Footnote [C]

*Importance—Plot and Situation—Spiritual Values of Story—
Order of Events—Introduction—Primary and Secondary
Events—Climax—Naturalness—The   End—Preparation—
Proportion—General Considerations.*

A story is the relation of what certain persons did in certain
places and under certain conditions of existence, and in its
broadest aspect the art of narration includes the description of
persons and delineation of character, the depiction of scenes,
and the suggestion of atmosphere. But these matters bulk so
large in themselves as to call for separate treatment. My
purpose here is to discuss constructive technique, how the bare
story, a succession and progression of events, should be
planned and built up before writing. The problem is
constructive, not executive, and should be considered and
settled, within limits, before setting pen to paper.

In fact, much of the technique of fiction writing concerns
matters of conception and construction. Giving the story its
verbal flesh after it is thoroughly mapped out in mind in accord
with the canons of the art is in truth a more or less simple
matter to the writer who has any command of language and
literary facility. The result may not be a masterpiece—which is
a significant idea, justly elaborated, and perfectly told—but it
will possess one of the elements of a story worthy to live. The
trouble is that so many writers set about the task of expression
when all they have in mind is the merest germ of an
undeveloped idea or story, and then are forced to wrestle with
construction and with language at one and the same time. Each
task is great enough for the undivided attention of the ablest
artist. I believe that in the end the constructive task is pretty
well done, but that the more strictly literary task to give the
conception verbally perfect expression is usually somewhat
slighted. We have so many well conceived and elaborated
stories, and so very few so perfect in expression that they

deserve to live, a fact indicating that construction can be learned by nearly all, though literary power seems to be incommunicable. The proper attitude for the beginner, who has not the facile practice of his art at his fingers' ends, is to treat the first draft of his story as merely tentative and an aid to development.

ORDER OF EVENTS

The discussion of plot and situation in the preceding chapter was pointed to emphasize the importance of the constructive phases of technique. A plot is not merely a climactic sequence of events or happenings; a plot is some human struggle, some conflict between opposed forces, that finds concrete expression in a climactic sequence of events; and an infinite number of persons and incidents may be devised to give specific expression to a single fundamental plot idea. Having fixed upon a plot, the writer of fiction should realize precisely what is the human problem or struggle involved, and should consider just what sort of characters and just what sort of incidents will give most effective, most interesting expression to the particular story idea. This he should be the more ready to do because a story usually comes to mind ready formed as a series of events, and only infrequently is the first combination the best, that is, the one which will present most forcefully the underlying plot, struggle, problem, or essential story idea. The writer of fiction has for material vast infinity of imaginable characters and imaginable events; he should manipulate that material to a narrowly specific end, the end of giving most effective expression to his particular story idea or plot. In other words, he is an artist, and must devise and re-devise, select and reject, arrange and re-arrange that with which he deals.

Another condition of his art requires the fiction writer to master the technique of construction and always to practice it before approaching his strictly executive task of writing. A story is usually more that a mere physical spectacle, more than a sequence of physical happenings. Each event, each situation is fictionally significant or interesting by virtue of its relation to the natures or spirits of the persons involved. Through the physical tissue of what happens runs the psychical thread of personality, relating part to part and rendering the whole indeed one story. A story is a thing of spiritual values as well as a physical spectacle, and it cannot be written adequately by visualizing its events and following them with the pen. Some part of its spiritual value rests in necessary implication from what happens, but not all. The rest must be brought out deliberately by the writer, and he cannot hope to do so to the full unless before writing he realizes the necessity and shapes his work accordingly. The point is of very great importance. It would be hard to overestimate the number of potentially fine stories that have been ruined through failure to realize that the main situations or happenings of each fiction could not have full effect on a reader unless many subtle matters of personality and spirit were deliberately brought out in advance.

The first concern of the writer who has found his bare story is to determine the order in which to cast both its major and minor events. The necessity that the more important happenings of the story be given some climactic arrangement, to hold and stimulate the reader's initial interest, has been touched upon before, but the general ordering of events is a matter of such importance that it will be discussed at length.

The aim of any story is to interest, and the writer should endeavor to touch his reader's interest as quickly as possible. Long, purposeless, and therefore dull introductions—usually the result of the writer's having set to work with no very definite idea of what he has to do—should be avoided; the writer should consider precisely what his story is, and then how he may best set it in motion without delay. The technique is easy to state but hard to meet. Perhaps it may be possible to set off with a happening sufficiently unique and striking in itself to arouse a reader's interest; descriptive touches as to setting or as to a character may be employed; or—after the fashion of some modern writers—one may indulge in a little philosophical overture forecasting the nature of the tale. A classification of the several ways to open a story might be made, but it would not be useful. In the first place, each good story is perfectly unique; in the second place, independent reading of fiction will show the ways much more completely than mere statement. One slight matter is perhaps worth noting. Often inherently dull introductory matter can be given piquancy on the lips of a narrating character.

The writer should not distort his story merely to begin it interestingly. The aim of fiction is to interest, but the person to be interested is the cultured reader, not the mere sensation-sop. If a particular story is forbidden by its content to begin with a rush, it should not be wrenched and distorted to that end. The writer who seeks merely to cater to current tastes with each tale will do well to devise fictions that will subserve his purpose naturally. Thereby he will achieve his aim the more easily, and may spare the reading public much inferior work. But it is always well to make quite sure that any story cannot be begun swiftly before adopting the more leisurely approach. Kipling's "Without Benefit of Clergy" might have been begun so much less invitingly by one less skilled.

The more complicated the plot, the more difficult it will be to arrange its elements justly. The events of the structurally simple story usually can be related in chronological order; one gives place to the other without effort or preparation. The story with a complicated plot is not so simple to order justly. In the structurally simple story nearly all events have a primary value; each is a definite step in the climactic ascension of the whole. In the story of complicated plot, on the contrary, there are a comparatively small number of events having this primary value in that they are definite steps in the climactic ascension, and there are also a comparatively large number of minor events having only a secondary value in that they serve to give the primary events naturalness, intelligibility, and effect. Thus, in the story displaying the conflict of two characters, the chief events will be those giving the struggle the most intense expression, and the minor events, having only a secondary value, will be those which serve to prepare the various conflicts and to build up and vitalize the two opposed persons. Even if these minor events are only secondary in intrinsic significance, they are essential to the story, and the task of its writer—no easy one—is to order its primary events so that they will form a climactic ascension in point of tensity and interest, and to order its secondary events so that they will function naturally in endowing the primary events with the fullest measure of significance to the reader.

Each story is unique and characteristic, and of course very little specific advice can be given as to the just ordering of events, primary and secondary. There are two main necessities; the story must be told, and it must be told plausibly. The first necessity, that the story be told, requires that the writer take care, not only to set forth its primary events with due elaboration, but also to develop its characters into individualized human beings—an office chiefly performed by the secondary events—and to make due preparation for each successive primary event, that the reader may fully understand its import. The second necessity, that the story be told plausibly, requires that the events be ordered naturally as well as climactically, be told in accordance with the canons of life as well as of art. The difficult task of the writer is to picture his single phase of life so deftly and with so little apparent forcing of his matter that the whole will be endowed with the significant simplicity of art and yet have the naturalness of life. Of course it is hard, and of course it takes long and patient practice to conquer the secret. That is why the writer who has full command of technique is so rare.

The story itself largely determines the order of its primary events, for their succession is the story. But the secondary events are as largely subject to the control of the writer, who may devise, adapt, and order them almost at will, and in just and natural ordering of them lies much of the secret of verisimilitude. They are the mortar that binds the stones of the edifice, and by slighting them many a fine initial conception has been rendered feeble in execution. They need not be elaborately treated; in fact, the technique to be acquired is to relate them in due subordination to events intrinsically more important, though giving them an easy and natural flow and succession. But the minor events must be ordered justly, that the story may march becomingly from major event to major event, and therefore the writer must struggle with their ordering. No rules capable of statement regulate the matter; the writer can only be told its importance and urged not to consider his story fully developed and ready for writing simply because he has determined the order of its main events.

Perhaps the whole philosophy of the ordering of events, major and minor, can be stated broadly to be that in ordering the more important events of a story the writer must regard chiefly the necessities of climax, that is, of art, while in ordering the secondary events he must regard chiefly the necessity to be natural, that is, to achieve verisimilitude. Art is life raised to a higher power, and the struggle of the artist is to present his phase of life as simply and pungently as can be done without entirely severing the relation between his conception and life itself.

One function of the secondary events of a story is to prepare the elements of the main events. In the love story, John meets Joan that he may subsequently make love to her. Another function of the secondary events is to develop character. In London's "The Sea Wolf" most of the earlier episodes and many of the later are narrated to build up the impression of Wolf Larsen's ruthlessness.[D] It follows that any minor event will serve a double purpose when devised and placed so that it will forward the mechanical progress of the story and also illustrate character. Tarkington, in "Monsieur Beaucaire," begins the story with a scene over the card table which not only gives the barber-prince his necessary introduction to society but also shows the stuff of which he is made. In constructing his story before writing, the author should select and place each incident with an eye to its serving as many purposes as possible. The story will gain thereby in compactness and uniformity of interest. It is golden advice to urge the writer not to accept the secondary events of a story as they first come to mind, but to re-arrange and re-devise until each happening performs as many functions as the necessities of the story permit.

There is nothing particularly new and striking about the main events and situations of many stories that not only are getting published to-day, but are truly interesting and worth while.

CHAPTER V - CONSTRUCTIVE TECHNIQUE OF NARRATION - 50

Their interest—and therefore their worth—derives from their writers' management of secondary events. By varying the nature and succession of minor events, any fundamental plot theme, such as the "eternal triangle" of two men and a woman, may be utilized a thousand times without essential loss of interest. As has been stated, the naturalness and plausibility of a story depend largely upon just selection and ordering of its secondary events, and, curiously enough, in a very real sense the reader's interest depends on the minor happenings. The plot must be a real plot and an interesting one, but, at the last of it, the plot is only the skeleton. The minor events of the story are the comely flesh that gives the conception the attraction and interest of life. The figure may be grewsome, but it is accurate. A thousand skulls look much alike, but no face is precisely the same as another, even to the casual eye. The flesh makes the difference, and the minor events of a story are its flesh.

The chief necessity in beginning a story is to begin it interestingly, if its nature permits; the chief necessity in ending a story is to end it—and there is no proviso as to its nature. A story is a fiction with a plot, and a plot is a chain of events with a definite and significant ending. The writer who has discovered or devised a true plot upon which to hang his fiction will not struggle on aimlessly after narrating the climax, for there will be nothing more to relate. I believe that absence of true plot is most often responsible for the story that stumbles to a lame and inconclusive halt—not an end—rather than executive inaptitude on the writer's part, for the climax of a true plot is a hard thing not to feel and realize. At any rate, when the climax is reached and the story told it must be ended, justly but finally. There is nothing more for the reader, unless the characters are caught in another chain of significant events. "But that is another story."

To recapitulate, a story is a progression of events, major and minor. The story largely determines the character and order of its main events, for they are the story itself; nevertheless the writer should give them climactic arrangement, as far as possible. The minor events are more subject to his control, and he should devise and order them chiefly with an eye to verisimilitude and plausibility, not forgetting that each should serve some definite purpose and will be the more useful if it can be made to serve more than one.

PREPARATION

Two sorts of preparation must engage the attention of the writer of a story. The first is purely mechanical, and is the result of the writer's realization of the physical necessities of his story. If at some definite point the hero is to be found in some definite place by other characters, the writer must prepare to place him there. The necessity is obvious, and this sort of preparation requires little discussion, except the warning that in the complicated story it will demand close attention. But the second sort of preparation is a much more delicate matter, and in a sense is a great part of the art of fiction. I have reference to the necessity that the writer individualize and vitalize the people of his story so that the significant situations of the fiction may have maximum effect on a reader. The problem is not so much how to delineate character, which will be taken up later, as to plan the whole story so that it will have body and not be a mere report.

There are three fundamental types of story, it is true, in that a story may emphasize any one of its elements of character, of complication of incident, or of atmosphere. But the story which depends for its appeal on the novelty or intrinsic significance of the bare succession of its events is somewhat rare; at least it is true that fiction concerns man primarily, and in the normal story, or, better, in the story which the necessities of plot-structure most frequently produce,[E] the man is as important as the event. Since the person is as important as the event, the persons involved in any significant situation of a story must be developed as well as the situation itself. The aim is to give the situation maximum effect, and the concern of the writer is not so much to develop character, strictly, as to give the body of reality to the whole story. It is about human beings, and, however novel and interesting the plot, unless they are given some of the vivacity and concreteness of real men and women the fiction will be devoid of the breath of life. The first sort of preparation builds up the physical situations of a story; the preparation now under discussion builds up its people.

Nothing is more common than for the beginning writer to devise or discover an eminently worthy plot idea, and nothing is more uncommon than for him to utilize it to the full and develop it adequately. The reason for the failure is simple. The better the plot, the more humanly significant its situations. They are so very significant, in the case of the fine plot, that the beginning writer is led to think that his only task is to outline them. But merely to outline a significant situation or event will not give it the emotional force that fiction must possess, otherwise the newspaper would be read in tears. The event must involve real people, if the emotion of a reader is to be aroused. A newspaper item may state that Mary Smith has committed suicide because deserted by her lover, but though the casual reader will realize intellectually and abstractly the pathos of the situation, his emotion will not be stirred unless he is a more sensitive human precipitate than most readers. To move his heart, rather than his mind, some particular Mary Smith, like no one else in the world, must walk a living presence through the story built about such a theme. The difference is between merely reporting events and picturing life.

Like most other matters of technique, this of giving individuality and life to the people of a story is based on the necessity to achieve verisimilitude and interest. Human life is a great complex of millions of men and women doing certain things, and in a story, which is a picture of a phase of life, the people must be drawn with as much definition and detail as the events, or the reader will not accept the fiction as fictional truth.

In great part, the matter of developing the human elements of a story is a problem of construction, as is the matter of preparing a natural succession of events. The writer first must order his main events as interestingly and plausibly as possible. He then must devise and order his secondary events as to give the requisite spacing and naturalness to the whole, and he also must take care to provide for such action on the part of the characters that when they come to the main events they will be something more than named abstractions. Of course, the writer has means at command to vitalize his people other than to draw them in actions illustrating their peculiarities, but it is difficult enough at best to vivify a character, and the writer who depends solely on his powers of direct description will achieve very meager results. I have already referred to the part the secondary events of a story play in developing character, and have cited London's "The Sea Wolf" as an instance. A great part of the book is devoted to a succession of episodes which develop Larsen's striking personality. It is very skillfully done in this respect, and the result is as memorable a figure as exists in recent fiction. The beginning writer and even the more practiced hand will do well to note the great part that just construction must have played in producing the impression of the Wolf's virility and ruthlessness.

It all may be termed a matter of drawing character, but the necessity is to realize that in constructing his story before writing an author must prepare for the development of its people as well as for the development of its events. The work will have to be done sometime, if the story is to be more than a report, and it should be done before writing, so far as it is a matter of construction. The writer who has conceived a plot of real merit has done much, but he has not done all. The striking events of a plot are significant only in relation to the people of the story, and a reader must be made to feel the reality of the characters as well as the reality of the events. The single concern of the writer of fiction is to lay on his page a picture of a phase of life that is effective because it is plausible, and he must give equal attention to the persons of the story and to what they do, both in construction and execution.[F]

PROPORTION

In planning his story with an eye to giving it the greatest semblance of reality, the writer has one means ready to his hand which is the more useful because somewhat mechanical. I have reference to the preservation of proportion.

Fundamentally, proportion is a mere matter of space or length. In real life events vary in point of the time they take to happen, and in the story proportion may be preserved by dividing the available space justly between the several events. Normally a love scene will take longer to happen than a murder, which is an affair of one high-pitched moment, and in planning and writing a story which contains both a love scene and a murder a proper amount of space should be assigned to each. In the story the reader passes through days in an hour and through hours in a minute; he must not be made to pass through minutes in an hour, and through hours of events as important to the story in a minute. A murder may be more important in the story than a love scene, and so require emphasis, but it cannot be stressed by great expansion without violating proportion. Emphasis must be laid by narrating vividly, a matter to be taken up in its proper place when discussing executive technique.

The mere fact that the writer must narrate the main events of his story in some detail usually will lead him unconsciously to preserve proportion so far as they are concerned. The space necessary to develop a murder will have roughly the same relation to the space necessary to develop a love scene as the duration of a real murder has to the duration of a real love scene. But the minor events of a story function on a different plane from its major happenings, and so cannot be proportioned similarly. If a murderer must sail from London to New York to reach his victim—either on account of the place necessities of the story, or to fasten an impression of his animosity on the reader—the minutes of the days of the voyage cannot be related with as much detail as the minutes of the actual killing. In planning a story, the writer should make provision for the secondary events and the strict matter of transition, as well as for the main events, but he should not plan to narrate in detail until a main event is reached. The beginning writer seems very often to be afraid to narrate in general terms, even where the story demands no detail, and the fault probably arises from a vague feeling that the reader will not accept the author's say-so, but must be "shown." To an extent, that is true. However, where the matter is of transition, merely to forward the mechanical progress of the story, detailed narration is distortion. It will inevitably cause loss of suspense and interest.

Realization of the relative importance to the story of each of its parts will give the writer the standard whereby to distribute its space. In writing the short story the preservation of proportion is most essential; there is so little space at hand that two words cannot be wasted in detailed narration where more general narration will suffice, and it all comes under the reader's eye so nearly at one moment that any disproportion in the treatment of events of equal importance will be detected. In the novel, lack of proportion may be a more secret fault, but it will have its effect.

GENERAL CONSIDERATIONS

In casting about for a story the writer should regard chiefly the intrinsic merits of each idea that comes to him. But when he has pitched upon his theme or plot, and approaches the task of construction and elaboration, he should change his viewpoint and strive to view his conception with the cold eye of a reader. A reader has nothing to go upon except what the writer sets down, and realization of the fact will lead the writer in construction to provide for every matter essential to give the story full appeal. Unless it is developed completely, it will fail to impress one who has no knowledge of the conception except that imparted by the writer's words. Nothing essential can be omitted or slighted without risking failure. On the other hand, nothing unessential can be brought out without obscuring the real story. Careful construction and elaboration of the initial idea is necessary before writing, that the author may have his hands free for the difficult task of execution, and in construction the writer should occupy the detached position of a reader when estimating what should be developed and what suppressed.

CHAPTER VI - EXECUTIVE TECHNIQUE OF NARRATION

Mode of Narration—First Person Narration—Variation—Advantages—Disadvantages—Plausibility—Third Person Narration—Advantages—Avoidance of Artificiality—Consideration of Length—Maintenance and Shifting of Viewpoint—Attitude of Author—Style—Product of Technique—Congruity of Manner—Story of Action—Fantasy—Story of Character.

After conceiving and elaborating his story, the writer must approach the task of expression. The two preliminary matters to be settled are the mode of narration and the manner or style for which the story calls. Though preliminary, they are most properly treated as part of executive technique.

MODE OF NARRATION

The question of how the story may be told most easily and effectively is much more delicate than merely to choose between narration in the first or third person, for numerous variations in these two basic methods are open to adoption. Each method or viewpoint has its advantages and disadvantages, and that method should be chosen which most nearly suits the particular story.

Variation in first person narration—the typical form of which is to have a chief character tell his own story—is possible by shifting the story from the lips of a major character to those of a less important personage, who is often little more than an animated mouthpiece. The device is really an attempt to escape from the inherent disadvantages of typical first person narration. A just regard for the reader often requires that more be set forth than any major character could naturally know, but some minor character may be made to pass ubiquitously through the whole tale, viewing the essential acts of all the major characters and relating them to the reader. Or the device may be carried farther, and the story told in the first person by a succession of characters.

The chief advantage in first person narration by an important or the most important character lies in the fact that the reader is accustomed to a more or less one-sided presentation of events. That is the way he sees things himself, as a bare succession of happenings springing from the conflict of human motives of which he can be sure only of his own. Something happens, and he knows within limits why he did his part in bringing it about, but the part of the other man is obscure to him, and he can go only on conjecture and inference. So the story told in the first person has perhaps a slightly greater flavor of plausibility than that told in the third person.

There is another advantage in first person narration. Some stories cannot be launched with a rush; the significant action must be prefaced by a considerable mass of introductory matter that is essential to full understanding of subsequent events; and this introductory matter can often be made less repellent to the reader when it is artfully introduced by a narrating character. The speaking character can be made to tell his story with a smack of personality that appears somewhat affected and flippant when the writer employs the third person. This flippancy and affectation is apparent is some of Kipling's and O. Henry's work, and probably repels as many as it attracts.

Generally, throughout a story, first person narration makes easier the attainment of uniformity of style, if that be a merit in the case of all stories as it unquestionably is in the case of the short story, with its necessary emphasis on all formal unities. During the vogue of the historical novel some years ago this mode of narration was ridden to death simply because it lessens for the writer the labor of catching what he conceives to be the tone of the particular society he is portraying. As to the general matter of tone, Stevenson refers, in a letter, to "The Ebb Tide," as "a dreadful, grimy business in the third person, where the strain between a vilely realistic dialogue and a narrative style pitched about (in phrase) 'four notes higher' than it should have been has sown my head with grey hairs." Had the story been told by one of the characters there would have been no difficulty of the sort.

"The Ebb Tide" probably could not have been told effectively in the first person, for much of its power derives from the way in which Stevenson limns the lovely South Pacific scenes through which its poor lost derelicts of people move. Their speech is "vilely realistic" because they are common men, sea captain and clerk and middle-class Englishman, and the lips of no one of them could have been made to state effectively without distortion what his eyes saw. Any story has certain matters which must be brought out justly if the whole is to have due effect, and if first person narration renders it impossible to treat such matters justly that mode of narration cannot be used. The example of "The Ebb Tide" shows that in estimating the availability of narration in the first person the writer must consider that the very nature and being of a character may seal his eyes to many matters. Moreover, the reader will not readily accept in a narrating character the literary power that is even expected in the author writing in the third person. A story is a whole, its people existing subject to the limitations of its necessities, and the mode of narration must function naturally with the rest, and not demand impossibilities.

One difficulty of first person narration is not so much fictional as psychological. If the story demands emphasis upon the good qualities of the narrator, his bravery, devotion, love, generosity, or a thousand others, a reader will soon weary of the eternal I. It is safe to say that if a character must be shown in a strongly favorable light, let it be done by the author or some other character, not by himself, unless the moral perfection of the person is a matter solely of inference from his acts.

The very complicated plot can rarely be handled well in the first person, particularly if the events cannot be cast in chronological order. On the other hand, first person narration is often a useful device to keep from the reader's knowledge, unobtrusively and without seeming effort, matters which he must not learn prematurely. Conan Doyle's Watson is an instance. Thus the chief disadvantage in employing the narrating character, that he cannot be made omniscient, may be turned to advantage. The whole question is one to be determined only after careful consideration of the demands of a particular story, and the chief need is not so much to state rules for its solution as to point out the real necessity that the writer know what he is about before pitching on a mode of narration. It is a prevalent habit, and a bad one, to accept a story as it first takes shape in the mind, narrative, point of view, and all.

There is a tendency among writers of fiction, particularly those who are just beginning, to narrate in the first person, perhaps because they feel that the reader will accept the story more readily in such shape. Other things being equal, first person narration is a trifle more natural and plausible than narration in the third person, but its limitations are much more strict. At the last of it, readers are so thoroughly habituated to the impersonal viewpoint that a writer does not gain much in power to convince by adoption of the other. A story is taken up because a story is wanted, and a reader is willing to accept the conventions of the art. So incredible a fiction as Poe's "A Descent into the Maelstrom" was probably best told in the first person, but the average story need not strain so sedulously for verisimilitude so far as the mechanics of narration are concerned.

Typical third person narration is illustrated by the story of action, the wholly objective story, told in the third person. The impersonal relator is omniscient, but his omniscience is not so obtrusive as in the story that touches on the facts of the soul. This omniscience of the relator is the chief advantage of third person narration, but the writer will only infrequently find it advisable to assume omniscience absolute and entire, involving knowledge of all the objective acts and the subjective motives of all the characters. If the story is largely analytical of more than one character the writer may be forced to "know it all" in order to display his material. But omniscience carried to such a point tends to be over-artificial, the underlying cause of much of the artistic weakness of the story which lays bare the souls of all characters instead of one or two of the most significant. In his own daily life the reader is accustomed to a one-sided presentation of the social spectacle, and complete omniscience on the part of the impersonal relator of a fiction has the taint of artificiality, or even of bare exposition. And exposition, which implies a mathematically complete presentation, is not fiction, which implies shading and suppression, absolute or temporary.

Any suggestion of artificiality may be entirely avoided, and the frequently necessary advantages of third person narration retained, by assuming omniscience as to all the physical facts or events of the story while rejecting omniscience as to the souls of the characters, except the souls of one or a few. Thus the writer may escape the inherent limitation of first person narration, that the story is told by a character of definite powers and knowledge, and retain the chief advantage of that mode of narration, the more or less single viewpoint, corresponding with a reader's own outlook on life and its happenings. This hybrid method of narration utilizes the virtues and rejects the vices of the two strict types. By telling his story in the third person, but from the viewpoint of one or two of the chief characters, an author may assume the desirable omniscience as to objective facts and the desirable limitation upon knowledge as to subjective motives. This is not to say that the nature of a particular story may not call for strict first or third person narration; it is merely a suggestion that the virtue of each type may be utilized at once. Each story makes certain demands, and the writer is not confined to two means of satisfying them.

A reader of any catholicity of taste can recall numerous examples of the various modes of narration, and in future reading it will be directly profitable for the writer to note the narrative device employed, and how it has aided or hampered the development of the fiction.

More extreme devices have been, and may be employed, such as Richardson's of telling a story in a series of letters. They are curious rather than important.

In estimating the availability of a mode of narration the writer should consider the matter of length. The adoption of the omniscient viewpoint may carry the story unnecessarily beyond due limits, for the writer who has taken to himself the privilege to know all facts and motives may be led into depicting events or analyzing character for his own pleasure, rather than because the story demands it. If a story demands space, space it must have, but the essence of literary power and artistry is to write with the utmost brevity and pungency compatible with adequate expression. The story must be told; every essential phase must be brought out; but unsignificant words can only do their bit toward spoiling the desired effect. The adoption of a too inclusive mode of narration may lead the writer astray; conversely, the mode of narration most nearly suited to the necessities of his story will aid in holding his pen to the line. If the story is of action, unconcerned with motives save by implication, and the writer tells it in the first person, or in the third person from the viewpoint of a single character, he will be led to confine himself to the depiction of the panorama of events, which is the work in hand. Yet, if the story requires that the reader be given a direct view of the spiritual workings of large numbers of characters, the writer must tell it in the third person and assume universal knowledge as to event and spirit. A mode of narration must be deliberately selected for each new story with due regard to its idiosyncrasies, and to make the choice correctly cannot fail to be of great advantage.

It is often stated that having settled upon what is most narrowly termed a mode of narration and most broadly a viewpoint the writer should be sedulous not to depart from it. The writer of the short story should not alter the narrative point of view, for obvious reasons. The short story is short; it depends for its power upon dramatic effect; and in writing it there is no occasion or excuse for any shifting of outlook. The short story is artistically the strictest form of prose fiction, that is, it is most strictly subject to the conventions of the art of fiction, of which maintenance of the point of view is one. But the novel is a much looser form, and unless the particular story is uniquely uniform in texture, as the frank tale of adventure, shifting the point of view often will prove necessary.

If the author of a novel has chosen to write with knowledge of the inner workings of more than one of the characters, but not with knowledge of all, so that he relates from the viewpoint of several characters, rather than the viewpoint of some impersonal observer to whom the souls of all are open, numerous shifts of viewpoint will be necessary. They are implied in the mode of narration itself. The world cannot be looked at through the eyes and souls of a succession of characters without a succession of shifts. All this merely amounts to saying that certain modes of narration which cannot be employed in writing the strict short story may be freely employed in writing the novel. In the case of the novel, or of the story that is somewhat brief without being a strict short story, the task is not so much never to shift the viewpoint, rather always to indicate the shift with clearness. Just as the reader's interest should be the first consideration in choosing matter and devising a plot, clarity to the reader must be considered when any shift in the narrative point of view becomes necessary. Let the shift be avowed and obvious; any uncertainty can lead only to confusion.

It follows that writers who have chosen to tell their stories from the viewpoints of several characters will prove the most profitable for study as to how to shift viewpoint without confusing a reader. Chiefly, of course, they are novelists, Eliot, Balzac, Hardy, Scott, and an infinity of lesser lights. Galsworthy, for instance, in each of his chapters succeeds in producing a singular unity of effect, with corresponding clarity for the reader, chiefly by making his shifts of viewpoint coincide with shifts of scene and person.[G]

Inextricably bound up with the mode of narration and the general narrative viewpoint of the story is the matter of the author's own attitude toward the story. The distinction between these matters is fine, but real. It is possible that a given story may be told, adequately so far as the bare story is concerned, in any one of several different ways. Narration in the first person by a major or a minor character may be employed, or the author may write in the third person, assuming knowledge of all events and of the inner workings of one, some, or all of the characters. But there is another consideration. The whole conception may depend for its appeal upon what I am forced to call very roughly sympathy for a character or group of characters, and a mode of narration must be employed which will enable the author to express his sympathy that he may evoke the reader's.

I do not wish to shift the discussion into the field of ethics, but the point is that any chain of events may be colored in the telling favorably or unfavorably to the persons concerned. A coarse instance is afforded by a prosecution for crime. In making their final arguments to the jury, prosecuting attorney and attorney for the defense alike deal with the same facts in evidence, but on the lips of one the defendant will be a glorified and persecuted saint. A more delicate instance is afforded by Stevenson's "The Ebb Tide," previously mentioned. Robert Herrick commits all the criminal acts committed by Huish, the cockney clerk, except to attempt murder, but the reader pities Herrick while hating Huish. This is so because Stevenson writes of Herrick with a measure of sympathy, and tells the story, though in the third person, almost entirely from his point of view. But of Huish we have only his acts and words. The treatment of him is wholly objective.

The story which develops a chain of events tending to show a character or group of characters in a strongly unfavorable light should not be told too objectively, or the reader will be repelled by its uniform ugliness, a matter which must be considered in choosing a mode of narration. It is not a point of morals, but one of contrast. If the writer has no sympathy for one or some of his people, or writes in such manner that he cannot express any predilection, they will appear all of a piece to a reader, with a consequent loss of interest. In this very real sense the story whose characters are uniformly repellent may be said to be bad art.

Generally, therefore, the writer must consider the necessities of his story in determining the mode of narration, and must also consider his own attitude toward its people and their doings. Its appeal to him may lie in his sympathy for some person or persons, and unless that sympathy be given expression in some way the story may not have an equal appeal to a reader. The perfect fiction is a congruous expression of a phase of life, and in it the more subtle matters of life, sympathy and predilection have their place.

STYLE

The term style has been so exclusively used to denote an author's style in general, rather than the style of some particular work, unlike the styles of others by the same hand, that it is apt to suggest something different from what is meant by its use here. To show the distinction I cannot do better than to quote from Stevenson's "A Note on Realism."

"Usually in all works of art that have been conceived from within outwards, and generously nourished from the author's mind, the moment in which he begins to execute is one of extreme perplexity and strain. Artists of indifferent energy and an imperfect devotion to their own ideal make this ungrateful effort once for all; and, having formed a style, adhere to it through life. But those of a higher order cannot rest content with a process which, as they continue to employ it, must infallibly degenerate towards the academic and the cut-and-dried. Every fresh war in which they embark is the signal for a fresh engagement of the whole forces of their mind; and the changing views which accompany the growth of their experience are marked by still more sweeping alterations in the manner of their art. So that criticism loves to dwell upon and distinguish the varying periods of a Raphael, a Shakespeare, or a Beethoven."

In the case of Stevenson himself this process is especially manifest. With a unique earnestness he sought from the first to adapt his manner to his matter, and, since he grew with the years, each new tale concerns itself with matter a little more humanly significant than its predecessor, and is told in keeping therewith. The result is that such stories as "The New Arabian Nights" series, fantastically conceived, fantastically told, give place to "The Master of Ballentrae," "The Ebb Tide," and "Weir of Hermiston," fictions worthy in every sense, the last, indeed, an unfinished masterpiece. And with each new story the author's style gains in dignity and restraint, in the process of adaptation to the work. I mention Stevenson in this connection not because he is greater than many others, nor his work finer, but because its range was so wide that it called for many manners or styles. All will prove a profitable study, for they are all Stevenson's and yet all different. Writers who have been somewhat more narrow in choice of matter have not been under so pressing a necessity to vary their manner with each new work.

Possibly it is unwise to emphasize the matter of style at all when writing for the apprentice author. Telling the story is usually task enough, and style in general is a product rather than an item of technique, therefore best sought indirectly. But even if the more delicate tones and shadings possible in writing are beyond the reach of all save the most skilled, preservation of the broader congruities of manner is possible by the beginner, and must be achieved if his work is to be even passable. Such a story as "The Scarlet Letter" could not have been told in Dickens' usual manner, nor could "The Pickwick Papers" have been written in the style of Meredith. The manner of telling any story must be reasonably adapted to its content, or the whole will be a shabby burlesque, destined never to achieve the laurel of print. The writer need not fret about his individual style, but he should ponder seriously the manner for which each story calls.

The story chiefly of action is best told without great verbal elaboration, which is unnecessary and tends only to hinder the march of events. The whole thing is an objective presentation, and the open character of its elements renders unnecessary laborious and involved explanation. The bare facts carry their own warrant openly displayed, and when they are shown the task is done. Sentences will tend to be a trifle shorter than in other work, and paragraphs likewise. The writer's chief aim will be to write not only clearly but vividly, for the story of action must depend chiefly upon vividness for its verisimilitude. The simpler figures will be profitable to employ, provided they are not too good and do not call attention to themselves rather than the image they are used to precipitate. The writer's general endeavor will be to follow stylistically the rapid movement of events. A reading of Dumas will show this method in use.

If there is a touch of fantasy about the tale, greater elaboration in sentence structure and some freakishness in the choice of words will be permissible and even desirable, for true verisimilitude lies in the accordance of manner and matter. The story with a thread of unreality in its essential composition will not gain in power by matter of fact telling; the measure of verisimilitude which it can attain is strictly limited by its very nature, and can be gained to the full only by frankly and avowedly making it what it is.[H] An instance is afforded by Stevenson's "New Arabian Nights" series or Hawthorne's "Tanglewood Tales."

The story placing emphasis on character, or the story of atmosphere, unless the atmosphere itself be the onrush of events, will normally demand more leisurely treatment than the story of action. The movement of the story will be slower, and the style will be correspondingly affected. Dealing with motives directly will force the writer to qualify and distinguish, adding to length of sentences, while to precipitate an atmosphere in words is a matter of such delicacy that the writer will be forced to employ every resource of language, with a consequent complication in structure. The necessity is to hold the tale in mind before writing until its totality of character is realized, then to strive to commit no gaucheries in execution. The right word for the right place must be sought, indefinite advice which will prove of little aid in writing a single story, but which will yield ample returns if followed through careful and intelligent writing of many stories. In dealing with this matter of manner or style, and the necessity that it be in keeping with the particular story in hand, it is impossible to give examples on account of lack of space. I can only refer the reader to almost any fiction that has resisted the tooth of time. To leave prose for a moment and turn to poetry, a reading of Milton's "L'Allegro" and "Il Penseroso" will demonstrate the possibility and display the result of adapting the manner to the matter. The style of both is unmistakably Milton's alone, marked by his dignity and elevation of tone, yet one is as sweet and light as a summer breeze, the other as grave and sombre as a minor chord.

A reading of Jane Austen will prove profitable in this connection. Her books are all of a piece in manner and matter. Perhaps the writer who must please the somewhat hectic modern market will find little profit in imitating her choice of matter, but the skill with which she weaves her pattern will be instructive. Emily Bronte's "Wuthering Heights" perfectly fits the garment to the body. The story is wild and its style is wild. George Douglas's "The House With the Green Shutters," a more recent book and one of singular power, is well done in this respect. It is essentially rugged and bitter, and the author, though without particular distinction of individual style, strikes no note not in keeping with the general conception.

CHAPTER VII - EXECUTIVE TECHNIQUE OF NARRATION

*Narration Method—Story of the Commonplace—Story of the
Bizarre—Vividness—Suspense—Emphasis and Suppression—
Matter of Weight—Expansion and Vividness—Primary and
Secondary Events—Transition—General Narration—Blending
of Elements.*

The writer who has discovered a good plot, so that his interest
will not flag in writing, and who has fully developed the
conception, so that he can have a single eye to execution, will
meet few obstacles in setting down the whole story. Difficulties
there will be in plenty, but they will be self-imposed. That is to
say, it will be very easy to give the justly elaborated conception
expression approximately adequate, but it will be very hard to
give the conception verbally faultless expression. If the writer
strives merely to tell the story, the labor of writing will be
slight; if he strives to write with artistry and power, it will be
infinitely great.

This book is on the technique of fiction writing, not on the
technique of writing; my aim is to discuss only the matters of
technique peculiar to the art of fiction. Thus, in this chapter I
shall have occasion to state that the important event should be
emphasized, and that vividness in narration is a means to that
end, but how to narrate vividly is a question of rhetoric
generally, and it is not my purpose to discuss it. Moreover, it is
emphatically true that the capacity to narrate vividly cannot be
attained by the mere study of examples, the only way in which
the matter can be studied. The writer can only strive constantly
in his work to write with definition and force. It is all a matter
of practice, whether or not the capacity must be inborn. But the
principle of fiction technique, that the important event should
be emphasized in some way, whether by vividness or
expansion, is subject to direct statement and to assimulation
from the direct statement. Therefore statement of the principle
is all that a work on fiction technique need attempt. The rest
lies with the writer himself.[1]

The first chapter on the executive technique of narration took up the two preliminary problems of the mode of narration and of manner or style; this second chapter has to do with certain other matters that must be considered in writing a story, viewed as a chain of events. Character, atmosphere, and dialogue will receive separate treatment, and for discussion of the strict technique of expression the reader is referred to works on rhetoric, except that in discussing the technique of description in the next chapter I shall have occasion to touch upon nicety of expression.

METHOD

The method of narration is necessarily influenced somewhat by the style the writer of a story strives first to find and then to maintain, but the style does not entirely determine the method, or the method the style. The matters are distinct, though mutually influential.

There are two kinds of lives, or at least two kinds of incidents, the humdrum and the bizarre. Likewise and consequently there are two kinds of stories to be told, the humdrum and the bizarre. Each may be fashioned into something worth while. Whether the matter of a story is worth while depends on the significance of the phase of life involved; whether the story itself is worth while depends on its plausibility or verisimilitude, which depends on the way it is constructed and told.

The humdrum story, that deals with the more common actualities of life, the little details that are significant only in combination or in relation to certain characters, can be told as simply as the writer desires. He has only to set down the succession of details that constitutes the story. Each new incident will not only advance the narrative progress of the story, but the commonplace nature of each incident in itself will tend to give the fiction its necessary plausibility. Simply because each incident is common and of universal occurrence the reader will accept it and the story compounded of such elements. Matter of fact phrasing, not phrasing too "literary" in spots, is most suitable.[J] Such a story does not require high lights of expression, and they should not be interpolated.

The story dealing with the strange and wonderful is another matter. In writing it the author's aim is the same as in writing the commonplace story, to give it plausibility and verisimilitude, but the task is infinitely more difficult. Proper construction will aid greatly, and in execution the writer has two resources.

The first is the method of Defoe, and consists in showing the reader the strange course of events through a lattice of familiar thoughts and things. It is an attempt to give the essentially bizarre story something of the plausibility and power of the story of the commonplace by interpolating universally familiar matters of detail. They are unnecessary to the bare story, but they are useful to give the reader a thread of connection between his own experience and the strange fiction. The method is persuasive, and requires a high degree of craftsmanship to employ well. Familiar and unfamiliar must be woven together with a careful and skilful hand. And obviously it requires space. Examples are Defoe's work—often cited—such as "Robinson Crusoe" or "A Journal of the Plague Year," or Balzac's "Peau de Chagrin."

The second method to give to the strange and wonderful verisimilitude and plausibility is not persuasive, but consists in writing with such vividness, definition, and force that the verbal picture will be accepted without question as visual evidence. Seeing is believing. In fact, the more strange or wild any chain of events, the deeper their impression on a reader, provided always that he be made to see them. Obviously, to the use of this method the highest powers are necessary, the power to select the salient and distinctive points of the thing to be drawn, excising all superfluous matters, the power to choose the exact and vivid word, and, finally, the power—more, seemingly, than that of mere word-selection—to precipitate reality in words, one sometimes manifested by works the diction of which is not particularly dynamic. It is the method of Stevenson and Kipling, among others, and to the author who can employ it no degree of novelty in the physical conditions of a story is a deterrent. He can show the thing like a painting or a stage scene, and his reader runs breathlessly with him, caught up in the race of events. The method demands the highest imaginative powers in the author, that he may actually see the matter he is depicting, in detail and in the mass, and the highest executive powers, that he may fix its living image with his pen.

This method to present the bizarre event with all the color and body of reality—of course it may be employed in depicting the commonplace as well, though expression of the commonplace should not be too heightened—is the method of the severe literary artist, because it is compatible with the most perfect unity and the greatest brevity. To arouse emotion in a reader the writer must have something more than mere color in his work, but to make a reader see anything it is only necessary always to search for the right word, which is the word both exact and dynamic. Yet if this is the sole condition, it is a doubly hard one. The perfectly exact word is so elusive, and, when discovered, it is so often lacking in the requisite force. Exactness is not enough; the needful word is the one that not only will fit the author's vision, but give it life; and it is here that figurative language finds its office. "I saw a fleet," is exact. "I saw a hundred sail," is equally exact, and much more vivid.

Vivid, direct writing, which does not depend on connection with his own experience to hold the reader, is the most practicable narrative method for use in the short story or novel of incident, that is, in the typical fiction, where interest centers in the course of events. In other words, it is the typical narrative method; the method of coaxing the reader into believing the strange by showing it in juxtaposition with the familiar is a variation from type. Narration consists in stating what happened. If what happened was commonplace, the reader need only be told it; if what happened was strange, the reader must be coaxed or forced to believe it, and the writer must either coax him or narrate with such vividness and power that the word will have the body and reality of the fact.

SUSPENSE

The term suspense is often misused to characterize a quality of narration supposed to result from the employment of some technical device. What is meant, of course, is that a good story, involving real people, justly related, will hold its reader's interest until the denouement is reached. Suspense means continued interest, and can result only from sound conception, careful elaboration, and adequate narration of a story. The reader who is shown real people in an interesting situation will be in a state of suspense through his curiosity and desire to learn what happened next. There is no technical device to create suspense, for suspense can result only from the worth of the whole story. I mention the matter thus briefly on account of the misuse of the term. If there is any technique to create suspense, it is the technique to order a story's events in a climactic ascension, and is not an executive device.

EMPHASIS AND SUPPRESSION

A story is made up of a succession of happenings, some of major and many of minor importance, and in telling it the writer must emphasize the most important events to impress their significance upon a reader. It will not do to relate the whole, indiscriminately, with as much vividness as the writer can command, for the fictional value of the whole necessarily resides in the relation between its chief events, and that relation can be made apparent only by showing them in high relief. The most important events of a story must be emphasized; events of some but not of controlling importance must not be stressed too much; and the very trivial events, which are usually matter of transition, necessary only to the mechanical progress of the story, should be suppressed by narrating without detail and in general terms.

Fundamentally, emphasis and suppression are matters of weight, while proportion is a matter of space. There is a real relation between preserving proportion and laying emphasis, but it is accidental. When an important event is somewhat complicated, as a love scene, proportion requires that it be narrated in detail, for it would take some time to happen in reality; and due emphasis will be secured by detailed narration. But when an important event is inherently simple in character and brief in the time it would take to happen, proportion requires that it be given not too much space, while emphasis requires that it be stressed. To stress such an event, the writer's sole recourse is vividness in narration. The physical details are few, but they must be made strikingly impressive. Where an event is essentially complicated, a knot of many details, emphasis may be laid by detailed narration, by expansion, and proportion will not be violated. In the case of the important but inherently simple event there are no great number of details to be marshalled on the page, and the writer can only strive to invest his few words with power.

The writer should consider the matter of proportion in allotting the space of a story before writing, as has been stated. In writing, the mere fact that he follows events in detail with his pen will lead him to emphasize by expansion, where the subject matter naturally calls for that mode of securing emphasis. Where expansion is impossible on account of the absence of details to be narrated, the writer's realization of the importance of the event will lead him to cast about for the vivid word. That is to say, in dealing with the important events of a story the way to write is to visualize the procession of happenings and to follow them with the pen in detail, seeking the vivid and emphatic word where the event is vivid and emphatic. When the event is a bundle of many details, setting them down will emphasize the episode by expansion; and where the event is simple, and a mere detail in itself, as a blow, vividness in narration will counterfeit the force of the episode.

Normally, the succession of chief events will take up the greater part of the space available for a story, and, if the work of construction has been done properly before writing, the writer will have his attention free to visualize each successive happening and to picture it. The difficulty will be to express perfectly. The process is natural. It cannot be too strongly insisted that the way to write the strict story part of a story is to strive to see the thing in imagination and to get it on paper with the breath of life in it. By following his vision with his pen the writer will take care of the matters of proportion and emphasis without detached calculation looking to that end.

But that is not quite true in narrating secondary events and writing general matter of transition, the part of a story that gives the main events a natural sequence and proper spacing, or that develops character. The main events exist only for the story; they are the story. The secondary events and matter of transition exist largely for the sake of the reader. Such events prepare the characters, for instance, that the main situations may have true and full dramatic value to the reader, while the general matter of transition serves to give the main events spacing and the story plausibility. And in narrating secondary events, and writing matter of transition, the writer cannot have an eye solely to imagining the procession of little happenings and to reproducing them in detail. If he wrote so they would bulk as large as the main events, and the short story would fill a novel and the novel an encyclopaedia. Instead, the writer must realize the reasons that led him to choose or devise each secondary event while constructing the story, and must narrate each minor event so that it will just perform its designed function and no more. The major events of a story are primarily significant, and it is sufficient to narrate them so as to counterfeit them as they would be in reality. The minor events of a story are not significant in themselves, but only in relation to something else, and in narrating them the writer should develop only their significant phases. They must be given reality and verisimilitude, but their aspects and implications unimportant to the story should not be detailed and thereby stressed. All aspects of the main events are to be detailed simply because all aspects of the main events are important to the story. They are the story.

The discussion is somewhat abstract and involved, but necessarily so. The technique will be easier to practice than it sounds, much easier, for instance, than to narrate the simple but important event with due emphasis through vividness. That necessity is supremely easy to state or realize, but supremely hard to meet in writing a story. The technique of handling secondary events and matter of transition is hard to state abstractly and to grasp from mere discussion, but when it is grasped it is comparatively easy to apply in writing, for it calls for no executive power, merely the negative power to leave out the insignificant.

It will be seen that the process of narrating the minor events of a story is not natural, but highly artificial. The process of narrating the main events is natural; it consists merely in imagining and reproducing them with as much body and color as possible. Where undivided attention to phrasing is most essential, the writer can give it; where it is least essential, in setting out a minor event, the writer must give much attention to what aspects of the episode he should emphasize. He cannot reproduce it in full detail simply for what it is in itself. Just narration of secondary episodes and transitional passages is a matter of calculation; just narration of the more important events of a story is a matter of warm creation and verbal power.

TRANSITION

In a sense, all events of a story may be said to have a primary value, for an event is at least a happening and has some interest for a reader. But the people of a story must be carried on from event to event, major or minor, and the story with them. The necessity causes the insertion of transitional matter in any story that has more than a single episode.

Transitional matter has no capacity to evoke interest in itself, unless it be so detailed as to form a succession of petty happenings, in which case it ceases to be strictly transitional. Therefore it should be gotten over with as quickly as possible. The writer should narrate in general terms, as has been stated in discussing proportion, the only end being to forward the mechanical progress of the story. No emphasis need be laid on such matter. A frequent fault in beginning writers is lack of capacity to pass from one event to another smoothly and swiftly. Many seem unable to step from detailed to general narration where the story demands it, and as a result their stories lose interest. The details of important events are the breath of life to a story, but details without fictional purpose only clog the action and discourage the reader's interest. Matter of transition should be handled as swiftly as can be done without rendering the whole story jerky and unbalanced. It may be noted that transitional matter on the lips of a narrating character can be given piquancy and made interesting in itself, like introductory matter.

Often transitional matter may be entirely omitted. Thus Maupassant, in "The Necklace," does not attempt to make the story an unbroken chronological progression. The nature of each particular story determines its content, of course, and where matter of transition is necessary or desirable the writer should realize its nature and handle it accordingly.

BLENDING OF ELEMENTS

Each story has two primary fictional elements, the people and the events, but it has three mechanical elements, the action, the speech of the characters, and the matter descriptive of persons or places. And while each tale is unique, and any one of these mechanical elements may largely preponderate over the others, nevertheless the normal fiction will devote a substantial amount of space to each. If the story permits—a proviso implied in discussing any matter of technique—it will be well for the writer to strive to distribute and intermingle its action, dialogue, and descriptive matter in a texture pleasing because varied. The whole should not be built of unwieldy chunks of description, speech, and action succeeding one another with monotonous regularity, but descriptive touches should be intermingled with the dialogue, and narrative matter with word-painting and the speech of characters. Obviously this is no absolute rule, and is perhaps not ever a matter of strict art, but it is true that a reader quickly wearies of much of the same thing, and a story is for its reader. Moreover, a story as a whole will gain in verisimilitude by judicious distribution of its mechanical elements. The matter is merely another phase of the necessity to give a fiction the seeming of life, and should not be neglected, the more so because it is easy and a mechanical matter. The beginner can afford to neglect no chance for success.

CHAPTER VIII - DESCRIPTION

Interest—Secondary Function of Description—Distribution—Story of Atmosphere—Effectiveness of Distributed Description—Description of Persons—Example—Analysis—Accuracy—Mechanical Limitations of Story—Use of All Senses—Description of Setting—Two Objects—To Clarify Course of Events—To Create Illusion of Reality—Use of All Senses Order of Details—Contrast.

All writing is descriptive, in a sense; narration, for instance, is simply the picturing of shifting physical conditions in a state of fluxation. But description is usually taken to mean the picturing of physical conditions more or less static. The term is used so here, for the technique of describing persons, scenes, and objects generally requires treatment separate from the description or narration of bare events. In describing a happening of his story, and in describing one of the characters, the writer's general object is the same, to show the person or event with the vivacity of life, but the conditions to which the writer is subject are somewhat different in each case. To mention but one difference, normally much more space is available for pure narration than for pure description. The events of a story are the story; its people and its setting are drawn only to give the fiction the highest attainable degree of verisimilitude. And, since the space available for description in the normal story is somewhat limited, the writer is under stringent necessity to make each word tell. In narrating an event, the matter has an interest of its own for a reader apart from the manner of telling, but in describing a person, scene, or object, the word is all in all. If the picture is not effective, nothing is achieved.

In coming to the writing of a descriptive passage, the writer should realize its secondary function in the story. Except in the case of the story of atmosphere, and perhaps of the story of character, a reader's interest will focus in the progression of happenings as such, and the sole object of strictly descriptive matter is to give maximum concreteness to the events by depicting their setting and individualizing the persons concerned. What happens is the first consideration, not where it happens nor whom it affects. Most stories might be told without a single word of strict description, and no such word should be given place in any story unless it will forward the fiction to a higher degree of verisimilitude.

It follows that descriptive matter should not be written pages at a time. Its function is to lend body and color to the whole course of events, therefore descriptive touches should be inserted throughout the whole course of a story. To give an itemized description of a character at the start, or to picture the whole countryside through which the story is to move, is a poor, because ineffective, way to write. Not only will the reader be repelled by great spaces of description, but he will forget the attempted picture with speed. The thing to do is to insert a vivid word here and there where it will do the most good as the story progresses. Description is for the story, not to give the writer a chance to heap words.

Numerous successful authors have indulged in lengthy descriptions, but the worth of their books does not result from the indulgence. Hugo's description of mediaeval Paris in "Notre Dame" is an example so extreme as almost not to be in point, but most of the elder generation of writers hampered the march of their stories by describing at inordinate length. No matter what the eminence of those who have written so, it is a technical fault, for it tends to render the story stiff and mechanical and unnatural. Lengthy description is not only inimical to a reader's interest; it is perfectly useless in a fictional sense. The sole function of description is to give body and reality to the story, and that function cannot be performed unless the descriptive quality runs through the whole, and the descriptive matter is not gathered into stagnant pools of words.

Much of the effect of the story of atmosphere may depend upon its descriptive matter, which may constitute a great part of the whole text. The fact does not invalidate the general proposition. In discussing the various aspects of technique, such as this matter of description, the initial assumption is that only the technique of the normal story will be stated. The normal story is the story of complication of incident, where interest centers in the course of events rather than in the people or the setting. Variants from it, the story emphasizing character and the story stressing atmosphere, by their very difference call for a different handling of elements.

Aside from the fact that a single lengthy description of a person usually will have less effect on a reader than the same amount of descriptive matter deftly interpolated throughout the whole story, or the fact that recurrent descriptive touches as to setting will do more to give body to the fiction than a single lengthy description, the writer should consider the mere rhetorical difficulty of descriptive writing. He must stand or fall by the picture he creates. In narrating, he has another resource than perfection in expression, for the bare event, apart from the way it is told, will interest a reader. But a picture will not interest unless it is a picture. Rhetorical skill is the sole determinant between absolute success and flat failure in describing. And it is hard enough to find one or two telling descriptive phrases without contracting with the reader to supply several pages of them. Not only is a long descriptive passage of questionable value in the normal story, even when well done, but very few can write a long descriptive passage well. The matter of emphasis here comes up again for consideration. Vividness is not absolute, but relative. One vivid phrase will seem vivid to a reader, but fifty or a hundred together will not. The reader will become accustomed to the higher level of expression, and the whole will fail of its object.

In the course of a story the writer will have occasion to describe persons and—roughly—things. Descriptive writing is descriptive writing, but the matters for consideration in describing a man or woman and a countryside are somewhat different, and will be taken up separately.

DESCRIPTION OF PERSONS

As I have stated in another place, the writer cannot gain much in capacity to express through the objective study of examples. He can only practice the art, seriously and intelligently. But Stevenson's brief story of an episode in the life of Master Francois Villon of Paris, poet, master of arts, and house-breaker, "A Lodging for the Night," so perfectly describes the persons involved that it calls for quotation. The object is not to display perfect use of epithet, rather to demonstrate the entire adequacy of brief and pungent description. Villon, after a short introduction, is discovered in a small house with "some of the thievish crew with whom he consorted."

"A great pile of living embers diffused a strong and ruddy glow from the arched chimney. Before this straddled Dom Nicholas, the Picardy monk, with his skirts tucked up and his fat legs bared to the comfortable warmth. His dilated shadow cut the room in half; and the firelight only escaped on either side of his broad person, and in a little pool between his outspread feet. His face had the beery, bruised appearance of the continual drinker's; it was covered with a network of congested veins, purple in ordinary circumstances, but now pale violet, for even with his back to the fire the cold pinched him on the other side. His cowl had half fallen back, and made a strange excrescence on either side of his bull neck. So he straddled, grumbling, and cut the room in half with the shadow of his portly frame.

"On the right, Villon and Guy Tabary were huddled together over a scrap of parchment; Villon making a ballade which he was to call the 'Ballade of Roast Fish,' and Tabary spluttering admiration at his shoulder. The poet was a rag of a man, dark, little, and lean, with hollow cheeks and thin black locks. He carried his four-and-twenty years with feverish animation. Greed had made folds about his eyes, evil smiles had puckered his mouth. The wolf and pig struggled together in his face. It was an eloquent, sharp, ugly, earthly countenance. His hands were small and prehensile, with fingers knotted like a cord; and they were continually flickering in front of him in violent and excessive pantomime. As for Tabary, a broad, complacent, admiring imbecility breathed from his squash nose and slobbering lips; he had become a thief, just as he might have become the most decent of burgesses, by the imperious chance that rules the lives of human geese and human donkeys.

"At the monk's other hand, Montigny and Thevenin Pensete played a game of chance. About the first there clung some flavor of good birth and training, as about a fallen angel; something long, lithe, and courtly in the person; something aquiline and darkling in the face. Thevenin, poor soul, was in great feather; he had done a good stroke of knavery that afternoon in the Faubourg St. Jacques, and all night he had been gaining from Montigny. A flat smile illuminated his face; his bald head shone rosily in a garland of red curls; his little protuberant stomach shook with silent chucklings as he swept in his gains."

The first thing to note about this fine descriptive fragment is that the persons are definitely placed in the room. The monk before the fire is the focal point; the others are placed in groups on his right and left hand. Two objects are achieved thereby; not only does the picture gain in definition, but it is given a closer relation to the story, which is partly concerned with what happens in the room. In other words, Stevenson describes his characters in relation to the story, and does not merely describe each one as he has occasion to name him, in isolation, and merely to give a reader a photograph with the name. Each is described in relation to the story and as he comes up in it.

The second thing to note is the extreme brevity and yet the complete adequacy of the description of each person. There is no itemizing of physical details; Stevenson has visualized not so much each man as the most striking characteristic of each man, and has used all resources of language to precipitate that characteristic in words. The result is impressive. A reader gains a clear and definite impression of the individual personality of each character, his spiritual nature as well as his physical aspect. The definition of the impression in each case results from the author's having described nothing possessed by any two in common. He has shown the unique quality of each person, which is all that is necessary.

This point of the technique of describing persons is nine-tenths of the whole technique. The fiction writer's proper aim is not so much to build up a physical picture of a character by itemizing the details of hair, complexion, stature, and so forth, as it is to reproduce the person's unique quality as an individual human being. Whether the character is an individual depends on the writer's creative genius, but whether he seems individual depends on his actions and the way he is described. Stevenson states Villon's salient physical characteristics, then remarks that the wolf and pig struggled together in his face, and a reader has the man, soul and body. The same method, though with less emphasis, is employed in picturing the others of the group.

A fundamental philosophical truth is that all knowledge is relative; we know things only in comparison with things previously encountered and classified. It follows that the difference between objects or persons is the ultimate factor that determines the character of each. The single unique quality of any character in a story is what the author must bring out in describing him if he is to have on paper the vivacity and distinction of the author's mental conception. In real life a reader meets many men and women; he does not take trouble to phrase the individual peculiarity of each, but he is acutely conscious of it. Each acquaintance stands for something unique and distinctive in his eyes, though he does not and perhaps could not state the essential difference from all others. And, in describing a person in his story, the writer must state that person's essential difference from all others, if the person is to have the reality of life for a reader, for the reader's only contact with the person is through the writer's words. In life, a reader will eliminate unconsciously from his mental representation of an acquaintance all qualities which the latter has in common with others, but verbal representation of a human being is shadowy enough at best, and in a story the writer himself must eliminate his characters' undistinctive qualities for the reader, or the persons will lack definition and concreteness.

The third thing to note about this example of the description of persons is a matter which it really does not illustrate, because it is perfect. My statement is at once obscure and paradoxical, but what is meant is that in describing a person it is possible to give so sharp a verbal etching that the reader will believe from the word itself. It is the descriptive aspect of narrating with such vividness that the word will be accepted as visual evidence. As it happens, in describing Villon and his fellows, Stevenson has found a combination of words which not only constitutes a vivid picture but is one that a reader may realize in imagination without loss of definition. Yet take such a touch as Balzac's in stating that a character had a face like a glass of dirty water. It is extremely vivid, but its vividness is somewhat superficial, that is, if a reader dwells on it, and tries to realize the image in thought, it will lose much of its definition. I have first-hand knowledge of the effect on only one reader, of course, myself, but others have confessed when questioned the same inability to realize this particular figure without loss of definition. The important point for the writer of fiction is that a reader will not pause to scrutinize too closely an image verbally definite and striking; such a descriptive touch as to a minor character will perform its office of giving the person vivacity and reality better than a more accurate but less heightened itemization of details. In a sense, Stevenson's passage is an example of this matter. It happens that his description can be realized without loss of definition. That is why it is perfect. But the same method may be employed less justly and yet have more effect than any mere itemization of physical details.

In picturing his chief characters the writer should not rely solely upon mere verbal sharpness. If the story is worth while they will have saliences that should be stated as well as exemplified in action. But the minor characters are shadowy enough at best, and any verbal definition that can be given them will lend concreteness to the story. If an image is not only striking, but also subject to realization without loss, so much the better. If an image is verbally happy, but not intrinsically perfect, it may be better to employ it than to write with just accuracy, but flatly. I believe that accuracy should be sacrificed to verbal felicity in no other place than in describing a minor character. It is an aspect of the general fictional necessity that mere literalness be sacrificed to verisimilitude, and, in describing a minor character, verisimilitude requires that a reader be faced by what will seem to him to be a definite person rather than some particular definite person. Strictly speaking, a minor character need not be individualized, but he must be drawn with the nearest possible approach to the sharp outlines of life. A major character must be drawn definite and unique; a minor character need only be drawn definite, though the more individual he is made the better. It follows that any sharp verbal image applied to a minor character will help the story, though it is within limits meretricious.

The three matters here discussed are the main considerations to be held in mind in describing the persons of a story. They should be described in relation to the story, as they are placed by their actions in the physical setting. In describing the chief characters, the persons whose personalities have significant relation to the course of events, the writer should endeavor to bring out with maximum definition and vividness the single unique quality of each person. In describing minor characters, the chief necessity is to give each person as much as possible of the definition and concreteness of life. Little space is available, and the writer may be driven to the use of somewhat meretricious figures. The perfect figure should always be sought, but, if the writer cannot discover it, the literally inaccurate figure may be better than flat writing. The general aim in describing persons is to give maximum concreteness to the whole story, and seeming definition will sometimes serve as well as actual definition.

The necessity that the persons of a story be described in relation to it, as they are placed in the physical setting, requires the writer to realize and regard the mechanical limitations of the story. If it is told in the first person, and the narrating character perceives another in the distance, a description of such other must confine itself to matters apparent at a distance, until the persons approach one another more nearly. The same necessity obtains where the story is told in the third person, from the viewpoint of a character who perceives another at a distance. Likewise, a character cannot be made to see through a house or a mountain, or into the next room. A good deal has been written on this matter, but from the wrong angle. The writer should not seek to master any abstract rule, rather should he strive to visualize his story as he writes it from the viewpoint from which he has chosen to tell it. If he thus gets into his story—so to speak—in describing he will unconsciously respect the mechanical limitations of the tale. Moreover, his attention will be free for the severe task of expression, undistracted by any eye to precepts. The way to write a story is to picture it in imagination and then follow it with the pen. That is why the unpracticed writer of high imaginative powers so often writes with a strict if unconscious regard for the laws of technique.

Another matter as to the description of persons is worth noting. The normal human being has more than the sense of sight; he can also hear, feel, and smell; and verbal appeals to these other senses may be effective. The timbre of a character's voice or sound of his step, the feel of his hand when shaken, an odor about him or her, as of liquor, tobacco, or perfume, may be stated in describing the person. Such a descriptive touch will often prove most useful, the more so because it gives another dimension to the person, so to speak. A very characteristic and impressive thing about Uriah Heep is his handshake, as Copperfield felt it. The matter will be taken up again in discussing the technique of describing setting, where it necessarily bulks larger.[K]

DESCRIPTION OF SETTING

The fiction writer is a dramatist in a very real sense, but he cannot depend for verisimilitude on flesh-and-blood actors, painted scenery, and actual properties. He must describe all these to give his narrative verisimilitude and concreteness. The technique of describing persons has been discussed, and the technique of describing mere objects, the properties of the piece, as the dagger in the hand of an assassin, is not so much a part of the technique of fiction writing as of the technique of writing generally. It is a question of rhetoric. But the technique of describing setting is fictional as well as rhetorical, that is, the writer of a story must consider what he should describe as well as how he should describe it. His task is more highly selective than the task of describing the persons or properties of a story. They, with the events involving them, are the story itself; the setting or environment of a story is not, but merely a background or stage. Yet sometimes, as in the story of atmosphere, the setting is an integral and necessary part of the fiction. One can only say that it all depends.

The fact that the setting is sometimes an integral part of the story and sometimes not requires the writer to set to work differently in each case. In writing the story of atmosphere, he must regard the setting as matter for reproduction for its own sake; in writing the normal story, he must regard the setting as only incidental, and should not reproduce it unless it will clarify the course of events for a reader or serve to give the story its necessary body and verisimilitude. The story of atmosphere requires separate treatment; here only the technique of describing the setting or settings of the normal story will be discussed.

As stated, in writing the normal story, the story where interest centers in the course of events, the writer should not describe setting unless it will clarify the course of events or lend body to the fiction in the eyes of a reader. General descriptive writing has no other function to perform. Realization of the truth will lead the writer to avoid writing great wastes of description. If a particular story requires that the physical conformation of a neighborhood be brought out, a few words will serve better than many, which will be apt to confuse a reader, at least to distract his attention. And when the writer describes setting to give body to the story, scattered descriptive touches will have more effect than a single isolated block of description. It is another aspect of the matter touched upon in relation to the description of persons. If a story is to have the concreteness, definition, and vivacity of life, the descriptive quality must permeate the whole, both as to the persons and their environment. The descriptive task cannot be performed once and for all, either as to the persons or the setting, any more than can the narrative task. Narration continues throughout the whole story, for it is the story; and likewise description must accompany each item of narration, for description is a part or quality of the whole story. Where the course of events is rapid, their quick succession itself will counterfeit a like phase of life, for an observer would note the events as such rather than the setting. But where the course of events is more leisurely, descriptive touches as to setting will be necessary to counterfeit such a phase of life, for an observer would note not only the happenings but the environment. A story is a reproduction of a phase of life; a reader is its observer; and the whole must be made to stand forth for him as a like spectacle would show in actuality.

The other necessity, to describe setting to give the story verisimilitude and concreteness, is not so easy to state or to meet. This sort of descriptive quality must permeate the whole story, as has been stated, and its introduction or creation is a matter of difficulty. The natural and best way to conquer the secret is to imagine the course of events while standing in the shoes of the person from whose viewpoint the story is told, then to follow them with the pen. Where the character would see, feel, hear, or smell something, state the impression upon him. Thus Kipling, in "Without Benefit of Clergy": "... Old Pir Khan squatted at the head of Holden's horse, his police sabre across his knees, pulling drowsily at a big water-pipe that croaked like a bull-frog in a pond. Ameera's mother sat spinning in the lower veranda, and the wooden gate was shut and barred. The music of a marriage procession came to the roof above the gentle hum of the city, and a string of flying-foxes crossed the face of the low moon." Kipling has imagined his story as Holden would have lived it; not only has he seen through Holden's eyes—he has heard with Holden's ears. In this short passage there are three appeals to the sense of sight, and two to the sense of hearing, and the fragment gains by stating more than visual impressions.

The point has been noted in discussing the description of persons, but is worth enlarging upon. The task to give body to a story is difficult enough at best, and the writer can afford to neglect no resource. Of the five senses whereby man grasps his surroundings, that of taste is probably of the least use to the writer of fiction, but the senses of sight, hearing, smell, and touch can all be utilized on occasion. A character at sea can be stated to have seen the waves of a storm, felt the force of the gale and the sting of driven raindrops, and tasted the salt spray, also to have smelt the musty fo'c'sle when he went below. Each touch will give the whole picture added reality for a reader. The beginning writer is too apt to rely solely upon what a character might have seen. A deserted house has a smell as characteristic as its look, and the fragrance of violets is as impressive as their visual beauty. Night can be told from day by its odor, and the rattle of typewriter keys in an office is as suggestive of modern industry as a serenade is of other days and other loves. A hero can feel his sweetheart's soft or toil-roughened fingers as well as see her expensive silks and furs or cheap and much worn dress. Life is a complex of many sense-perceptions, and the more numerous and varied the fleeting impressions a character is stated to have caught, the more concrete and real the story will be for a reader.

Description is the usual but not the happiest term to denote the general process of giving a story a setting and environment of its own. It is—or should be—more than a process of picturing scenes. All pertinent and striking sense-impressions received by the characters should be stated, for only thus can the nearest approach to a just representation of life be made. The writer's sole object is to give the fiction the concreteness of life; it cannot be achieved by painting verbal pictures for a reader, but it can be achieved by stating justly the ways in which the totality of the environment affected the characters. Just description of the characters will make them real men and women for a reader, and just statement of the effects of their environment upon them will make them real people in a real world.

The strictly executive technique of descriptive writing is not hard to grasp, however hard it may be to find the desired word. The impression that the character involved would receive first should be stated first, and the less striking details should follow in the order of their impressiveness. Thus, in describing a skating scene, the observant character should be made to see the interweaving skaters and to hear the peculiar whinnying ring of the skates before he sees individuals. It is all a matter of visualizing, or, better, visualizing and living the story in the shoes of the character from whose viewpoint it is told. The writer who will live each story thus in imagination, and will state the successive impressions the character would naturally receive while moving through such a chain of events in real life, will do far better work than one who strives to carry in his head a body of rules and precepts and to write with observance of them. Technique cannot be discussed without directly stating principles, but the business of actual writing is natural, not mechanical and artificial. The writer becomes artificial precisely when he forgets he is writing a story and begins to daub in descriptive matter without relation to the characters or the events. The thing to do is to get inside the skin of the character from whose viewpoint the particular story or particular part of the story is told, to see with his eyes, hear with his ears, smell, taste, and feel with his nerves, and to state no impression as received by him that the course of events would not allow him to receive. A horse-thief fleeing from a posse will have no eye for the beauties of a landscape. If the writer desires to show the scene for the sake of its contrast with such an event, he must do so lightly and quickly. A reader will be mounted with the pursued man, and his eyes will be ahead.

As to the matter of contrast between event and setting, no rules can be stated. All that can be said is that sometimes it is a useful device. But the main purpose of descriptive matter in the normal story is to give it concreteness, and generally the purpose will be realized best by stating the sense-impressions which would be received in actuality by the characters. A story will gain much in naturalness and plausibility thereby, for the same reason that narration in the first person or from the viewpoint of a single character is the most natural and plausible way to write, if the particular story permits.

One other thing may be useful to note. In describing a person, the writer should strive to state his unique quality as an individual; in describing a scene, also, the writer should seek to bring out its unique quality. That quality should be sifted out and realized in imagination, and then the writer should search diligently for the few telling words that will precipitate it. As the story moves on, men, women, and children, houses, ships, and electric cars, streets, deserts, and smiling fields, will come beneath the writer's pen. And they must all be given reality, not for their own sakes, but for the sake of the story.

CHAPTER IX - SPEECH

Potency of Dialogue—Mechanical Distribution—Naturalness —Directness—Dialect—Situation—Three Resources to Meet Demands of Situation—Physical Effect—Ellipsis—Elements of Language—Style—Verbs of Utterance—Transcription of Speech for it Own Sake—Creative Process.

When the writer of a story is not using narrative or description, he will be transcribing the speech of his characters. And in the matter of transcribing speech the writer of fiction has a chance comparable with that of the dramatist and the practitioner in the graphic arts. The effect of narrative or description upon a reader is secondary and derivative; the effect upon him of written speech or dialogue is very nearly primary. The fiction writer has not the actor's studied tones to give dialogue complete life and body, but the appeal of written speech is infinitely more direct and compelling than that of any other sort of writing. A word is a word, whether spoken or written, and cannot be read without setting up some echo in the ear. When the writer of a story describes its hero, a reader may or may not see an image, faint or distinct, behind the words. But when the writer sets down his hero's words, a reader cannot choose but hear. Even if the words be unnatural and stilted, they will be heard. That is why badly managed dialogue is so potent to ruin a story. The speech of the characters in a story is strongly impressive, whether for good or ill. The more powerful a tool, the more damage it will do if mismanaged.

Thus the essential force of dialogue or written speech may be a handicap or an assistance. If a character's words jar upon a reader, they will do so strongly, if they are natural and in keeping with the whole conception of the person, they will do much to give him the breath of life. It follows that the writer of fiction should give due attention to the transcription of speech, the more so because superficially the task is easy.

Perhaps the first consideration is the mere mechanical distribution of dialogue. In real life only the after-dinner speaker talks at inordinate length. Conversation, except that of the bore, is essentially fragmentary. Not only is each person's part fragmentary, but the whole conversation is usually somewhat brief. People caught in a more or less rapid sequence of events have no time to talk at length, and a story is a more or less rapid sequence of events. The writer must counterfeit a like phase of life with his story, and to do so he must mingle the mechanical elements of the story in a texture pleasing because varied. The mechanical elements of a story are its narrative, its description, and its dialogue or speech of the characters; these must blend and intermingle, varying the appeal to a reader and simulating the pattern of life. An unfailing sign of the amateur, at least of the amateur with no innate sense of fictional values, is a story made up of hard and angular blocks of narration, description, and dialogue. The skilled writer—if the particular story permits, a proviso always to be understood—will intermingle speech with action and description with both. Dialogue should no more be written pages at a time than should description, and if a great deal of speech must be transcribed en bloc, it should be broken up to some extent by descriptive touches and even by narration more detailed than that part of the story naturally calls for.

The next consideration is to make the people of a story talk naturally. The necessity has affiliations with the necessity that the speech of any person be made characteristic, for dialogue is an efficient aid in the portrayal of character. The writer must make each person talk like a human being, even if not like some particular human being. Good, nervous dialogue will be full of elisions, mere exclamations, unfinished sentences, gaps that a reader will bridge readily for himself. He will be skilled in the business, for that is the kind of talk addressed to him every day. In more sedate and leisurely ages, if we may judge from the tales then written, people could frame a sentence on the lips, but it is a lost art now. To be "literary" in transcribing speech is to invoke almost certain failure. "Literary" dialogue usually is ruinous. A reader's interest may survive stilted and affected narrative or descriptive writing, for most readers have read so much of such writing that it is almost expected, but stilted and affected dialogue will kill interest once and for all. In narrative there is something behind the word for the reader, even in description there is a faint something, but in dialogue there is nothing at all. The word is the word; if it fails, the failure is total.

Yet it will not do to be quite literal in transcribing speech. If the speech of real life is broken and fragmentary, it is also impossibly wordy and purposeless. The lawyer who has spent weary hours in reading transcripts of testimony knows the fact to his cost. The writer of fiction has not space to set down with minute accuracy just what his people probably would have said during the progress of the story; he must counterfeit the auditory impression of real speech by eliding and leaving sentences unfinished; but this mechanically broken and abrupt speech must have the purpose and direction which is wanting in real speech. The characters must not only talk naturally; they must say certain definite things and convey definite and necessary information, directly or by implication. There is little need to emphasize here the necessity that the writer have some fictional purpose in making a character say something, except to warn against transcribing speech solely for the sake of its suppositious intrinsic wit or vivacity, for each story will assert its own claims over the talk of the characters.

The question of dialect has been debated often and at length, both for and against. There are many fine stories in dialect in whole or in part, but their merit does not result from the employment of dialect, though the dialect may be a necessary part of some of them. In the larger sense, the question is merely one of naturalness. The pronunciation of no man is in exact accord with the ideal standard of the dictionary; all have mannerisms of speech and accent. In some sections such mannerisms are so common and marked as to form a dialect, almost a patois, and, if a story involves a character from such a district, fidelity to fact requires the writer to write dialect when the person is speaking. Dialect in a story must be intelligible to one unfamiliar with it, which requires the writer to iron out its greatest divergences from the normal in an endeavor to retain its piquancy while avoiding its obscurity. The question is not one of technique, but one of material. The only insistence of technique as to dialect is that it must be intelligible.

Unquestionably there is prejudice against the story told wholly in strongly marked dialect by a narrating character, both on the part of editors and readers. The type had a vogue some years ago, but its commercial and artistic defect is that it tends to be unintelligible.

Dialect is a useful aid in characterization, as is any slighter mannerism of speech. The matter will be taken up in discussing the portrayal of character. Here I am concerned only with the more general aspects of the management of dialogue.

As stated, the first necessity in writing dialogue is to place the word where it would be spoken in life, during the action, not in isolated masses of speech. The second necessity is to write naturally, and yet to invest the hasty and elided speech of the characters with purpose in the fiction. Dialogue must be not only natural and easy; it also must be significant, significant in relation to life—which is the matter of naturalness re-stated—significant in relation to the characters, and significant in relation to the story. That is to say, the justly written bit of dialogue will be natural, will illustrate character, and will inform a reader, directly or by implication, of something he must know if he is to catch the full savor of the story. These are the most general conditions to be borne in mind in writing dialogue. It remains to discuss the necessity that a writer consider the matter of situation while transcribing speech. The necessity requires discussion. Not only is it stringent, but it is politely ignored by too many books on technique.

The abstract statement is that the same person will talk differently according to his situation at the moment. Jones is Jones, of course, but the Jones who discusses preparedness with Smith is a different Jones from him who telephones to summon the doctor for his dying child, and his speech in each case will not be the same. My lady will not berate her maid for a fault as she will reprove her lover, and the head bookkeeper talking to a subordinate and to the boss would impress a listener as two different persons. The man and his speech are influenced by the event. The writer of fiction, being under constant necessity to counterfeit life, must keep the speech of his characters in accord with the situation as well as with the general looseness of actual talk.

It may be said that this necessity to write dialogue with an eye to the situation of the persons is merely a more narrow phase of the general necessity to be natural. That is true. The writer will never go astray who lives his story in imagination and sets down the speech of the characters as it would have been phrased in actuality. The only trouble is to determine just how the persons would have spoken, and it is a trouble because it requires more than a vivid imagination. Imagination will embody the course of events for a writer, will touch in the setting with glowing color, but imagination alone will not supply the words spoken. To find them, the writer must employ his intellectual faculties as well as his imaginative powers, and precisely for the same reason that the characters must employ their intellectual faculties in speaking. One who writes a story lives vicariously, lives another's life for the time being, and where that other would be forced to think, as in speaking, the writer must think likewise. Where the other would be forced only to observe, as in witnessing events or observing setting, the writer can rely solely on his imaginative powers.

There will be little difficulty in meeting the demands of the situation that is casual and commonplace. Speech that is merely easy and natural is adequate. If the incident is not particularly significant in a dramatic or emotional sense, the way that the character would talk in such circumstances is not hard to find. The story requires that a Southern gentleman of the old school welcome a stranger to his house, let us say; it will not be hard to find the host's words on that occasion. But suppose he must discover a few pages farther on that the stranger is his daughter's seducer. What will he say? The writer must find for him words that will chime with the tensity and dramatic value of the situation. To meet the necessity the writer has three resources.

The first lies apart from the matter of speech. By just portrayal of the physical effect of such a discovery upon a character the writer will accomplish much. To put it flippantly, the character will be made to talk naturally by making him speechless. To put it justly, in such a heightened moment in a story narration should be very detailed, and the writer should show the physical effect of any discovery upon a character before transcribing the words born of the moment.

The second resource of the writer to meet the necessity that a character's words fit the emotional and dramatic qualities of a situation is largely mechanical. Even casual speech is elliptical and exclamatory; speech born of excitement or agony of soul is strongly so. The more broken and fragmentary the character's speech, the greater the suggestion of emotional stress and upheaval.

The third resource of the writer is a matter of diction. English is a language compounded of Anglo-Saxon and Latin and Greek elements. The primary basis of the tongue is Anglo-Saxon; that is why it is English, and not a Romance language. We learn the simpler, less abstract part of our vocabulary, the part that stands for fundamentals, in childhood; the rest is acquired later. Not only is the Anglo-Saxon word the word we know best; it is also the word which will express our deepest loves and dreads and hates. The Latin element of the language gives it its flexibility and its capacity to express ideas, but its capacity to express emotion resides in its Anglo-Saxon element. Love, hate, birth, death, God, devil, father, mother, sister, brother, sin, lust, greed, filth, hope, care, weep, laugh, smile—all are strictly English words of Teutonic origin, and all are much more forceful and suggestive or connotative than any Anglicised Latin equivalents. The writer of fiction should realize the fact, and should make his people use strictly English words when caught in a pregnant situation. A lawyer, in discussing a case, properly may be made to employ the word deceased, for instance, but when informed that his wife has died suddenly, "Dead?" he should be made to say, "Dead?" That is very obvious, of course, but it will serve for an illustration.[L]

The question of character intrudes here. All speech should be characteristic of the person uttering it, but the necessity that the word should fit the moment is more stringent than the necessity that the word should fit the person, provided that the moment is so tense that its force might be expected to strip any husk of mannerisms from the persons involved. Indeed, the more strikingly individual the casual speech of a character, the greater will be the effect of making him utter in a crisis the broken and disjointed English words that come to the lips of all of us when our loves or our pocketbooks are threatened.

After stating the necessity to make dialogue accord with situation, and after pointing out the three resources of the writer to this end, a word of caution may not be out of place. In all human probability the writer will have for the significant situations of his story a much keener feeling and appreciation than any reader. There is some danger that the writer's feeling for his own situations will lead him to make his people talk a thought too brokenly for acceptance by a reader without the same keen appreciation of all the emotional and dramatic values of the situations of the story. The danger cannot be overcome by toning down the dialogue; the writer must force a reader to feel the power of all the situations of the story. In other words, dialogue in tense situations must meet the fact of situation, and each situation itself must be built up for a reader by proper development and adequate writing of the whole story. The art of fiction is a whole, as a story is a whole, and perfect handling of one element alone of his story, as the dialogue, will avail the writer nothing.

In transcribing speech, the less the writer thinks about the style or manner in which he has chosen to tell the story the better. The first consideration is to be natural, that is, to write as some real person would talk, and, if possible, to write as some particular person would talk. But the general tone of the story must be considered. The necessity is less stringent or nonexistent in writing the novel, with its permissible variety of texture, than in writing the short story of unity of effect. If the people of a story are super-normal, their lips must not drop banalities. That is a matter of character. But if the single effect sought to be produced by a story is of horror, for instance, its people cannot be permitted to make remarks that will hinder the attainment of the effect, which is a matter of preserving the general tone of the story. The speech of the characters must be in keeping with them, in keeping with the significant situations, and in keeping with the story as a whole.

There is one point about the management of dialogue which should be the less neglected because it is purely mechanical and very easy. A page of dialogue should not present to a reader a monotonous succession of "he saids" and "she saids," simply because the reader will feel the repetition and some of the illusion of the story be lost. The verbs characterizing utterance are infinite in number; moreover, it is frequently possible to set down nothing but the words of the speaking character. Thus Henry Sydnor Harrison, in "V. V.'s Eyes.":

"'Did she hurt herself?' said Carlisle, third-personally, to the elder girl, who had suspended her game to stare wide-eyed. 'What on earth is the matter?'

"The reply was tragically simple:

"'A lady stepped on her Junebug.'"

"Sure enough, full on the vestibule floor lay the murdered slum-bug, who had too hardily ventured to cross a wealthy benevolent's path. The string was yet tied to the now futile hind-leg. Carlisle, lingering, repressed her desire to laugh.

"'Oh!... Well, don't you think you could catch her a new one, perhaps?'

"'Bopper he mout ketch her a new one mebbe tomorrow, mom ... Hiesh, Rebecca!'

"Moved by some impulse in her own bouyant mood, Carlisle touched the littlest girl on the shoulder with a well-gloved finger.

"'Here—Rebecca, poor child!... You can buy yourself something better than Junebugs.'

"The proprietor of the deceased bug, having raised her damp dark face, ceased crying instantly. Over the astounding windfall the chubby fingers closed with a gesture suggesting generations of acquisitiveness.

"'Is it hers to keep?' spoke her aged sister, in a scared voice. 'That there's a dollar, mum.'

"'Hers to keep ...' replied the goddess, smiling."

Dialogue so managed is infinitely more natural and fitting than the he-said, she-said sort. Of course, the more characteristic the speech of the characters, the less the need for verbs of utterance. The primary office of such verbs is to indicate the person who is speaking, and, if the words spoken do that, the verb may be omitted. The secondary office of verbs of utterance is to characterize the manner of speech, and here it is well not to be too extreme. A character may snarl or bellow or invite or plead, for instance, but if he is made to flame in words there will be a suggestion of strain and artificiality for a reader. Intelligibility and suitable—not unsuitable—variety should be the writer's aims in managing dialogue.

The total amount of dialogue any story will contain depends on its nature and character. Possibly it is true that the more strictly dramatic a story, the greater will be the proportion of dialogue to the rest of the text. At any rate, a writer should never transcribe speech at any length simply for its own sake in an endeavor to trick a reader into thinking that the story is livelier than it is. Dialogue is attractive to a reader, but it is attractive in a story only when it is an essential element of the story. The writer should not depend on the intrinsic wit and vivacity of his characters' speech. Even if it is interesting in itself, apart from the story, the fact will not help the story as such, for a reader's attention will be distracted from its movement. Mr. Dooley's talk is beautiful, read apart and by itself; thrust into a short story, it would hurt the tale.

Finally, a word as to the actual creative process of writing dialogue. The way to narrate is to live and see the story's happenings in imagination; the way to describe is to feel the totality of the story's environment or setting in imagination as some character or characters must have felt it; and the way to write dialogue is to be each speaking character in turn for a space, and to write as the particular person would have spoken. As stated above, the writer will have to think as well as to imagine. He will have to comprehend the essential nature of each speaking character, his personality, education, and habits of life and mind, in order to discover the words that would be called forth from such a person by each new event. The task is not easy. But the writer should bring his full powers to bear upon it, for the dialogue of a story is tremendously effective, whether for good or ill.

CHAPTER X - PORTRAYAL OF CHARACTER

*The Three Modes of Characterization—Dialogue—Action—
Description or Direct Statement—Aims of Characterization—
To Show the Nature—To Show the Man as a Physical Being—
Character and Plot—Characterization by Speech—
Characterization by Statement—Characterization by Action.*

Characterization is an unlovely term, but it stands for much. In fact, it stands for so much that it is the hardest point of technique to discuss adequately. In the fiction writer's vocabulary, it stands for things as diverse as the necessity that the whole action of a story be significant in relation to character, and the necessity that the persons of the fiction seem real and individual, apart from any unique quality of their actions. Whether the action of a story is significant in relation to character depends upon whether the writer has discovered a real plot and developed it properly; whether the persons of a story seem tangible and unique apart from their actions depends upon the writer's skill in describing them and transcribing their speech. That is to say, characterization is a matter accomplished by narration, by description, and by the transcription of speech. A reader of a story has a clue to the natures of its people in their actions, in their words, and in what the writer has to say about them.

It may be well to enlarge somewhat on the respective functions of the three modes of characterization. Dialogue, action, and description or direct statement by the author all serve to give the character concerned individuality in the eyes of a reader, but all do not function in precisely the same manner or to precisely the same end. A few illustrations will make this clearer.

Suppose a story involving a character whose most salient trait is cruelty. The author may demonstrate this quality in the person by stating directly that he is cruel, by showing him in wantonly heartless actions, and by placing on his lips words which only a cruel man would utter. So far, so good. Each sort of demonstration will add something to a reader's realization of the character. But more is necessary. Cruelty is not a particularly unique trait; moreover, if a trait is unique, merely investing a character with it will not serve to give him the solidity and liveliness of a real person. Whether cruelty or any other trait is brought out, if it alone is brought out, the person will be a disembodied moral attribute rather than a man or woman. To secure a maximum effect upon a reader, the writer must manage to show some particular cruel person rather than a cruel person. And he must resort to the same means employed to show the strict character-trait, description or direct statement, dialogue, and action. But the writer's aim will be different. He will be concerned with the person's appearance and effect upon an observer or listener rather than with his nature. As Stevenson did for Villon in "A Lodging for the Night," the writer of a story involving a cruel person may call him a "rag of a man, dark, little, and lean, with hollow cheeks and thin black locks," or may employ any other combination of words that will give a definite picture of the man, viewed merely as a physical object, whether he be thin or fat, ruddy or pale, tall or short. And, in setting down a cruel person's speeches, the writer not only may make them cruel in content, but also may make them unique and individual by some mannerism of speech.

What I am trying to show is the fact that characterization, as the term is commonly employed, includes description as well as the strict portrayal of character. I have taken up the matter of the description of persons under that head, and I shall take up, in this chapter, the matter of speech as both illustrating character and individualizing the person. The whole difficulty of discussing technique lies in the necessity to treat in isolation matters which are influential in numerous directions in a story. In the latter part of this book I am following the conventional mode of discussing separately the matters of description of persons, dialogue, and the portrayal of character, but only after much pondering whether such treatment is advisable. The advantage is clearness; the disadvantage is loss of relation between matters mutually influential. For instance, writing dialogue is descriptive writing in a very real sense. A reader of a story stands in the position of an observer of certain persons. Their mannerisms of speech, which come to him through the ear, serve to build up his total impression of them as much as their physical appearance, which comes to him through the eye.

The process of characterization, then, however accomplished, is the result of two very different aims on the part of the writer of a story. The first aim is to show the essential natures of the people of the fiction, and may be attained by illustration in action, by direct statement, and by transcribing their speech. The second aim is to make them appear real men and women, apart from their natures, and may be attained by description— which is direct statement—by transcribing their speech, and even by action. In all three matters of narration, description, and dialogue the double process may go on. Narrating a character's victorious fight with a bigger man will leave on a reader a twin impression of the person's strength—a physical attribute—and courage—an attribute more strictly of character. When Stevenson, describing Villon, states that the wolf and pig struggled in his face, a reader is made to see the cruel sensuality of the man's face as a physical object, and to feel the cruel sensuality of his nature as a spiritual fact. If an avaricious character is made to make a miserly speech, a reader will have a clue to his nature; if he is made to make it with a lisp or stutter, there will be a descriptive touch as well. Characterization may be accomplished by narration, by description, and by dialogue, and characterization, as the term is commonly used, includes the description of persons as physical objects as well as the strict portrayal of character.

The writer of fiction who seeks to acquire the technique of characterization should note two facts. The sort of characterization which consists in displaying the essential spiritual natures of the people of a story is largely a matter of plot, of the sequence and character of each person's actions. If the writer states that John is miserly, and puts miserly words on his lips, the reader will never believe in John's avarice if he does a generous thing in the story. Actions speak louder than words. A reader will believe in John's avarice from the writer's mere statement and John's words, if John's actions are not significant adversely to the trait. In other words, personality and event must have true relation, on account of the inherent nature of a plot, a matter previously discussed. The second fact for the writer of fiction to note is that the sort of characterization which consists in giving the people of a story the vivacity and concreteness of real men and women is superficial but extremely important. A story is concerned with the spiritual natures of its people; it shows their growth or decay; the process is the story itself, particularly in the case of the story of character. But a story does not deal with disembodied moral attributes. It deals with men and women, and, if it is to be effective, a reader must receive some definite physical impression of each person as well as a knowledge of his nature. In the whole philosophy of fiction writing, characterization, as commonly understood, functions thus: the natures of the several major characters are primary elements of the fiction, as are the events; the impression an observer and listener would receive from each person must be built up for a reader that the fiction may have the concreteness and reality of life for him.

Speech, direct statement, and action, the several means whereby characterization in its two aspects may be accomplished, now may be discussed.

CHARACTERIZATION BY SPEECH

As indicated, characterization is a double process. The writer endeavors to reveal the natures of his people and to individualize them in a more superficial but equally important sense. Their speech may be made to reveal their spiritual natures, and it may be made to individualize them.

The process of making speech reveal character strictly is not difficult in itself, though it may be difficult to do so unobtrusively. A sentimental man will reveal his sentimentality when he says sentimental things, just as a hypocrite will reveal his hypocrisy in hypocritical words. Cruel words will reveal cruelty in the person who utters them, and generous words will indicate that their speaker is generous. So far as possible, the speech of any character should have relation to that phase of his character which is significant in the story. The cruel man may be avaricious also, but, if his cruelty and not his avarice is the trait which has influence upon the events of the story, his words should reveal his cruelty rather than his avarice. The content of his speeches should indicate his possession of that trait of his character which is influential as to the events of the story.[M]

The difficulty will be to find a natural place for these indicative speeches. The primary necessity in fiction writing is to be unforced and natural, and a character cannot be made to say words indicative of his inner nature unless he would naturally utter them under the influence of the circumstances of the moment. Here, again, the way to write is to get into the skin of the person involved, to live the story vicariously in his person, and, when events would naturally call from him words revealing his pertinent trait, to transcribe them. Primarily, a story is a story, and its writer must meet all its necessities within its limitations.

Lack of space forbids giving examples of the revelation of character by speech. Dickens will prove a profitable study in this connection. The words of Pecksniff, for instance, reveal as much of the soul of Pecksniff as we need to know. All good stories, in greater or lesser degree, display the method in use.

The second use of his characters' words to the writer of fiction is to individualize them. It is not a matter of content, but one of manner. Irrespective of what the person says, the way he says it, if unique, will serve to increase the definition of a reader's conception of him. If a character is made to stutter, he will gain in actuality and concreteness for a reader. The instance is coarse, but will serve to indicate what is meant. Dickens is unrivalled in his capacity to employ this device, although the writer of a short story or relatively compact novel will meet difficulties in following Dickens' technique of characterization. The "demmit" of Mantalini, the "dispoged" of Sairey Gamp, the greasiness of Chadband's words, the rounded periods of the immortal Micawber give a reader the greater part of his idea of each person.

This sort of characterization may well be called description. The aim is not to reveal the person's inner nature—though the content of a mannered speech may do that, of course—but to add to the definition and reality of any attempted picture of the person by calling in the sense of hearing. Unlike the effect of descriptive words on a reader, the effect of written speech is nearly primary, though it lacks something of the freshness and impressiveness of the spoken word. Writing descriptive of a character and his mannered words function together to individualize the person for a reader. The people of a story must be made to appear to be real men and women, if the fiction is to have its necessary verisimilitude and consequent effect, and mannered speech will do much to invest the speakers with reality.

The process must not be carried beyond the bounds of naturalness. A mannerism of speech may be too pronounced, in that it tends to arrest a reader's attention and distract it from the flow of the story. Unnecessarily distorted spelling, for instance, employed in an attempt to be too strictly phonetic, will call attention to itself rather than individualize the speaker, that is, it will destroy the illusion of the story. "Yuh" for "you" is an instance. We all "yuh" more or less, I think, and for the writer of a story to insist thus pedantically on strict phonetic accuracy tends to make the whole fiction labored and unnatural. The whole trick is to suggest any particular distortion, and yet to have the words as intelligible for a reader as if the spelling were normal.

Mispronunciation, of course, is not the only mannerism of speech that may be availed of. In fact, the tendency is to abuse it. An open ear toward the casual talk he hears will give the writer many useful hints, and so will reading the work of others.

The speech of class and class varies, as does the speech of man and man. A lawyer in a story should be distinguishable from a sailor by the very content of his vocabulary. So should a doctor from an engineer or a brakeman, or a musician from an artist. But it must all be done naturally. The writer cannot drag in by the ears technical terms of any profession solely that a reader may be informed indirectly of the speaker's profession. But a doctor or lawyer, for instance, will generally be in a story because it requires the presence of a lawyer or doctor, and therefore the story will offer opportunity for him to reveal his place in society by his speech. Incidentally it may be noted that this matter emphasizes the necessity that the writer of fiction be observant in life and omnivorous in reading. He should know the manner of speech of any considerable class of men. It is true, of course, that no two lawyers talk precisely alike, but it is also true that it is possible to suggest a lawyer speaking by a proper choice of words, and that is the thing to do, naturally and unobtrusively. If the speech of a character is individualized in some manner, and if, in addition, a reader can gather his business or profession from his words, he will gain much in reality and definition.

The content of the talk of the characters of a story, then, should reveal their inner natures, and their idiosyncrasies of utterance and word-choice should be devised and set down to intensify the impression of their individuality initiated by the writer's strictly descriptive touches. Characterization is a double process, and neither aspect of it should be neglected, whether the writer is narrating, describing, or transcribing speech.

CHARACTERIZATION BY STATEMENT

So far as characterization by direct statement is a matter of individualizing the persons of a story as mere physical objects, apart from their inner natures, it has been discussed in stating the technique of the description of persons. It was there stated that the writer's endeavor should be to catch and fix in words the most salient attribute of the character. And usually it will be the case that a person's most striking physical attribute will have relation to some fact of his spirit, as in Stevenson's description Villon's sensual face hints of his sensual soul. The fact serves to make more obvious the truth that characterization is a double process of individualizing superficially and of revealing the person's nature, and Stevenson's description of the medieval French poet is an instance of how the writer of fiction may attain both ends in a single phrase, and avoid the suggestion of artificiality in directly stating that a character is good or bad or brave or cowardly, as the case may be. Instead of stating that Villon was sensual and cruel, Stevenson states that the wolf and pig struggled in his face. A reader sees the man's face and comprehends his nature, and comprehends the spiritual fact the more thoroughly because reaching it inferentially from a mere picture. The point is worth noting.

However, the writer of fiction frequently must state his characters' moral attributes directly. Not all conceivable persons wear their souls in their faces; if some ruddy, bluff old gentleman is a villain at heart, the writer can only say so, unless he is willing to depend wholly on the revelation of spirit worked by the character's deeds. And sometimes such a revelation comes too near the end for the other purposes of the story. Much of the interest or suspense of a tale may depend upon the reader having knowledge of the natures of the people who struggle with one another singly or in groups. Or direct statement as to a character's nature may be necessary to emphasize the significance of his acts. Stevenson's "The Ebb Tide" is an example. The book is concerned with the unavailing struggle of a weak man to be other than weak, and the author prefaces the course of events with a thumbnail biography of the weakling that invests the progress of the story with something of the inevitability of fate. The method is a favorite one of Stevenson's, and is employed in most of his longer work. Each brief sketch is directed to bring out the character's trait or traits of significance in the story, and the whole fiction gains point thereby. Turgenieff composed a biography of each of his characters to deepen and clarify his own realization of them, and incorporation in a story of a swift and significant sketch of a character's previous life likewise may serve to deepen and clarify a reader's realization of the person.

Stating directly that any person is good or bad or brave or avaricious may give a reader a key to his acts, lending them point, but direct statement is the most infirm mode of characterization. Any mere statement is less impressive and less compelling than a demonstration. And direct statement of a character's nature must be reinforced and proved by his words and deeds. It is difficult enough at best to invest a fictitious person with reality, and the writer can afford to neglect no device.

As in fulfilling all other necessities of his story, in characterizing by direct statement the writer must be easy and natural. The requirement is somewhat indefinite, as stated, but real. Statement should not be too bald; a little subtlety will be profitable to employ. To state that a character is bad, simply, is too childlike, unless the story is told from the viewpoint of a child. The matter of viewpoint must always be considered in characterizing by direct statement, for obvious reasons. If the writer takes the position of an impersonal observer, to whom the souls of all characters are open, he can write pretty much as he wills. If he writes from the viewpoint of a single character, whether in the first or third person, he cannot assume too inclusive knowledge of the souls of the others. The matter has been discussed elsewhere.[N]

CHARACTERIZATION BY ACTION

The value of action as a means to give a reader realization of the physical appearance of a character is somewhat slight. To show the person as performing a feat of strength will suggest that he is a powerful man, but physical prowess is not a visually definite quality. Powerful men are not always even large men. Action is greatly useful to reveal the soul, but not very useful to reveal appearance.

However, between narrative and strict descriptive writing a borderland exists. A person may be described as having a sneaking look. That is strict description. But the writer also may relate how the person slunk down an alley to avoid meeting someone he dared not face. The descriptive value of the word "slunk" as to the person will be as great as the narrative value of the word to the event. It is merely the matter of vivid and effective narration approached from a new angle. Narration consists in stating what happened to certain persons and what they did, and a descriptive quality, both as to the persons and the events, should permeate it. Visualization of the story in imagination will show the way.

If action is the least effective way to hint of the characters' appearance, it is by far the most effective way to display their natures. The whole purpose of the story of character is to display the fact and demonstrate the consequences of the possession of certain traits by a group of persons or even by one person. And in any real story, that is, in any fiction built about a plot, the traits of a character and the events will be mutually influential. Either the characters will be devised to develop the events, or the events will be devised to develop the characters. The moral quality of an act is a sure index to the moral quality of the person who commits it. A story must reveal character simply because it consists of a series of events involving and produced by men and women. The writer's endeavor is not merely to narrate the events for their own sake, but also to realize just what sort of people must inevitably have acted so under the given conditions, and to employ his subsidiary means of characterization so as to bring out no trait unnecessary to the events.

There is one exception to the rule that the writer should endeavor to bring out only the traits of character strictly material to the events. Of course, the primary necessity in fiction writing is to develop the whole story naturally. But a story is for its readers. To give some stories full effect upon a reader it is necessary to invest one or more of the characters with a trait or traits not strictly necessary to the development of the story. Usually the aim will be to awaken the reader's sympathy that he may follow the fortunes of the person or persons with greater interest than the bare content of the story would evoke. For instance, if a story shows a character whose unlovely traits lead him into difficulties, investing him also with some pleasing attribute will deepen a reader's interest in his fate by arousing active pity for him. I have touched upon this matter before and from another angle in discussing the necessity that the writer select a mode of narration which will permit him to express his sympathy for a character that he may evoke a reader's. Stevenson's treatment of Herrick in "The Ebb-Tide" was instanced, and one who has read the book will recall that its author gave Herrick attributes of mind and soul more pleasing than inefficiency and weakness, though weakness was the single quality demanded in Herrick to render inevitable the course of events.[o]

No specific technique of characterization by action can be stated; it is a matter of conceiving and elaborating the whole story justly. The fact for the writer is that a person's acts reveal his inner nature, and the necessity that the writer must meet is to devise events and characters having a natural and plausible relation. If this is done, the essential substance of the story will be sound, at least, so far as character is concerned. Then the writer must meet the other necessity to make his people appear to be real men and women apart from any distinction of their inner natures. If both necessities are met, a reader will be faced by real people doing things for real and adequate reasons, which is a great part of the art of fiction.

All the acts of a person's life, great and small, would reveal his whole nature. But a story usually does not take a person from birth to death, and, if it does, it is concerned with a phase of the life rather than with the whole life. The art of fiction is highly selective, and necessarily so. Not only must the writer of fiction produce his effects within a limited space, but he must consciously eliminate here and suppress there in order to make apparent the real significance of his picture of life. The significance of one man's life may lie in his constant loyalty to and sacrifice for his family; the significance of another's in his complete disregard of his obligations as a husband and father. In either case, the writer who sees material for a short story or novel in such a life must select for reproduction chiefly those acts of the character which are significant as to the trait sought to be brought out, otherwise the story will be without point and meaning. Viewed superficially, a story is a mere string of events that happened to happen, a thing easy to write without forethought and calculation. But the truth is that a story is a chain of events at least influenced and sometimes even determined by character. If the influence of character in the fiction is predominant, it cannot be written justly without careful weighing and selection of the incidents that suggest themselves to the writer.

Having conceived a plot and devised characters to enact it, or having conceived characters and devised a plot to develop them, the writer should outline the main course of the story, mentally or on paper. He then should realize definitely and precisely what traits of character are primarily significant in the story, and should prepare to develop them so as to reinforce the effect of his people's acts upon a reader by characteristic dialogue and description and direct statement. The writer should consider next whether a due regard for a reader's interest requires that he invest his people with attributes not strictly necessary to the main events of the story, and therefore not to be revealed by each person's part in such events. Finally, the writer should realize that he must give each person a definite physical presence and illusion of actuality, and should prepare to do so by visualizing them in imagination. If all this is done at all, it is certain that the story will be a better piece of work than if the writer set to work with only a vague prevision of the course of events as his material. And if it is done justly, and the writer has adequate executive powers, the story will be worth while, at least in relation to character.

CHAPTER XI - ATMOSPHERE

Definition—General Atmospheric Value of Fiction—Tone of Story—Preparation of Reader for Climax—Examples—The Story of Atmosphere—Short Story—Setting—Slight Dramatic Value of Type.

Atmosphere—as the term is used by the writer of fiction—is a most indefinite word; it may be well to preface discussion of what it stands for by a definition. And in defining it is often conducive to clearness to state what a thing is not before stating what it is.

In the first place, atmosphere is not setting, although the setting of a story may aid in producing its atmosphere. The frozen wastes of a sub-arctic region or the man-made squalor of a slum may operate powerfully to produce on a reader of a story placed therein an impression of desolation or of misery, but that impression will derive from something other than the setting, and will merely be reinforced thereby. If a slum story is essentially cheerful and light-hearted in content, its reader will not be oppressed by the setting, however truthfully touched in, unless the writer deliberately makes his people seem miraculous in point of their capacity to avoid the contagion of their surroundings. The young girl in "The Dawn of a To-Morrow" is an instance of what is meant by the qualification.

Atmosphere is not setting, nor is it anything at all that is in a story. It is not the quality of the environment; it is not the general quality of the people or their acts; it is not the quality of the theme or plot. What is it? It is the general emotional impression made on a reader by the whole story. It is nothing that is in a story; it is the emotional effect produced by the story on a reader. Just as a scene, an event, or a person, unless very commonplace, will have some emotional effect on an observer, any story that is told so as to create the illusion of reality will have some emotional effect on a reader. As Stevenson said to Balfour: "I'll give you an example—'The Merry Men,' There I began with the feeling of one of those islands on the west coast of Scotland, and I gradually developed the story to express the sentiment with which the coast affected me."

A distinction should be noted here. "The Merry Men" is a strict story of atmosphere; its author, as he implicitly states, started with an emotional effect, or "sentiment," and devised only such persons and action as would deepen on a reader the emotional impression initiated in this case by the setting. But, as has been stated, any story told so as to create the illusion of reality will have some totality of emotional effect on a reader, apart from its specific emotional effects in various parts, unless the fiction is very commonplace. That is to say, the strict story of atmosphere, which has been touched on briefly in discussing story-types, subordinates its action and its people to its totality of emotional effect; in the normal story, whether it stresses personality or event, atmosphere, or totality of emotional effect on a reader, is a subordinate consideration, resulting from the necessity that an observer of persons and events be affected thereby in some general way. At least it is true that the writer of a story of complication of incident or of character cannot permit any consideration of atmosphere to interfere with the events in the first case or the persons in the other. Whatever totality of emotional effect may reside in his work will be inherent in the conception, as it would be inherent in such a spectacle for an observer, if the story should happen in actuality.

The sensible—because the most profitable—way for the writer of fiction to fit the matter of atmosphere into his general artistic philosophy is to disregard it entirely, except where it constitutes a primary consideration, that is, except in relation to the strict story of atmosphere. The reason for this cavalier treatment of the matter has been brought out. If any story is told so as to create the illusion of reality, some general emotional effect will be produced on its reader, will be inherent in the conception, as it would be inherent in the spectacle, if actual. It all comes down to this: by telling his story justly as a course of events involving real people in a definite environment, the writer will produce on a reader whatever totality of emotional effect is inherent in the conception. If there is no totality of emotional effect inherent therein the writer cannot produce it except by changing the whole conception and writing a different story. In the case of the strict story of atmosphere the writer's attitude is different. He sets out, not with a story, but with an emotional effect, and devises people and events and setting to produce it.

The point can be made clearer by more specific discussion. Assume that a writer has conceived a story with a definite plot, involving definite people, set in a New England village. Anybody who knows New England or has read Alice Brown or Mary E. Wilkins Freeman can testify that such a story, justly told, will have a definite and peculiar atmospheric value. But its atmosphere, its totality of emotional effect on a reader will be inherent in its setting and people, perhaps even in its events. The story itself will determine its atmosphere, which can be only the peculiar impression that a New England village, its people and their lives, produce on an observer. By choosing to write such a story, or by choosing to write any definite story, a writer debars himself from creating any atmosphere not involved in the story selected for writing. On the other hand, if a writer desires to put together a story of atmosphere, he starts with an emotional effect as the basic conception, and then casts about for a setting, people, and incidents that will produce such emotional effect. It all depends upon what the writer starts with. If he starts with an emotional effect, he may narrate any course of events, and draw any sort of people, and place the tale in any sort of setting, provided only that events, people, and setting be such as to produce the desired atmosphere or effect. But if the writer starts with a definite story, the only atmosphere he can create thereby is the atmosphere inherent in the conception.[P]

Though it is true that a writer may and should disregard the matter of atmosphere in writing a story which he has conceived as a definite course of events involving definite people, since any atmospheric possibilities of the fiction will be inherent in the conception and will be realized by telling it justly as to people, events, and setting, nevertheless a qualification must be stated. No story is conceived as definitely as it is written; the writer first grasps the plot or main situation, perhaps also the characters, and then expands the outline into a congruous presentation of a phase of life by filling in details as to environment, people, and events. This filling-in process may and should be performed partly at least before writing, but even if the writer postpones it until he is wrestling with the problem of execution, he must remember one thing. Any story has a general tone, largely determined by its climax or main situation. This tone or key of a story is not its atmosphere strictly, perhaps, but the dividing line between the two matters is very faint. The atmosphere of a story is its general emotional effect upon a reader, and its tone is very nearly the same thing, being the result of its writer's having justly performed his selective task by transcribing only such matters as harmonize with the main situation, tragic or comic. And a writer must regard the matter of the tone of a story in developing and writing it, if it is to have the significant simplicity and unity which alone can give the fiction maximum power and effect.

The practical problem can be stated most simply thus: a reader's intelligence and sensibilities must be prepared for the crisis, climax, or main situation by incorporating in the story only such matters of environment, personality, or event as harmonize with the emotional character of the main situation. The necessity is most stringent, of course, in the case of the short story, but it is a consideration to be borne in mind in writing any type of fiction. It is merely another aspect of the general question of preparation, which has been touched upon before. The situations of a story must be prepared in a mechanical sense, that is, the writer must prepare to place his people where each situation demands that they be placed; the people themselves must be developed and individualized, that the situations may have full dramatic value; and the mind and heart of a reader of the story must be prepared for the climax, which is the whole story in little.

If the main situation of any story is essentially tragic, it will never do not to hint the fact until the climax is reached, when a reader will be overwhelmed, rather than upborne and stimulated, by the torrent of battle, murder, or sudden death. The opening scene of "Macbeth" presages the lurid character of the whole play, and serves to key reader or spectator for murder. Likewise, in the case of a story essentially light and happy in content, the purpose of the writer is to develop and present one of life's many attractive phases, and that purpose will be defeated or at least hampered if woebegone people and unpleasant situations are given place in the fiction.

Considerations of contrast may lead the writer to incorporate in his story matter out of keeping with its general tone and main situation, but the effort is really to emphasize the general tone by striking a few discordant notes. Contrast is too delicate a matter to be discussed with any profit; whether or not the device shall be employed in any story is a problem that only the artistic sense of the writer of the particular story can answer.

It is very easy to say that a story should be told so as to prepare a reader for the climax, that he may accept it, yet, in a sense, the thing can be achieved only by adequate practice of the whole art of fiction. The general necessity is to make the whole course of events seem real and actual; the more specific necessity is to give a reader a definite clue to the nature of the story, that he may not be shocked into disbelief by the climax. This must be done unobtrusively, as every other technical device must be employed, under penalty of failing in its office.

A quotation showing effective employment of the device will not be useless. Stevenson's short story "Thrawn Janet" leads up to an encounter with the devil, and the author loses no time in preparing a reader for the entrance of his satanic majesty. The story begins thus:

"The Reverend Murdoch Soulis was long minister of the moorland parish of Balweary, in the vale of Dule. A severe, bleak-faced old man, dreadful to his hearers, he dwelt in the last years of his life, without relative or servant or any human company, in the small and lonely manse under the Hanging Shaw. In spite of the iron composure of his features, his eye was wild, scared, and uncertain; and when he dwelt, in private admonitions, on the future of the impenitent, it seemed as if the eye pierced through the storms of time to the terrors of eternity. Many young persons, coming to prepare themselves against the season of the Holy Communion, were dreadfully affected by his talk. He had a sermon on 1st Peter, v. and 8th, 'The devil as a roaring lion,' on the Sunday after every seventeenth of August, and he was accustomed to surpass himself upon that text both by the appalling nature of the matter and the terror of his bearing in the pulpit. The children were frightened into fits, and the old looked more than usually oracular, and were, all that day, full of those hints that Hamlet deprecated. The manse itself, where it stood by the water of Dule among some thick trees, with the Shaw overhanging it on the one side, and on the other many cold, moorish hill-tops rising towards the sky, had begun, at a very early period of Mr. Soulis' ministry, to be avoided in the dusk hours by all who valued themselves upon their prudence; and guidmen sitting at the clachan alehouse shook their heads together at the thought of passing late by that uncanny neighborhood."

Here Stevenson loses no time in keying his reader to the general pitch of the story. It is a task that the writer of any story must undertake. The general nature of the tale should be suggested as soon as possible, and the story should not be allowed to falsify its introductory hints, but should reaffirm them constantly, until all the divergent strands of the fiction are knotted together in the climax, which will need no interpretation. Take another instance from Stevenson, the beginning of "Markheim," where Markheim murders the dealer in curios.

"'Yes,' said the dealer, 'our windfalls are of various kinds. Some customers are ignorant, and then I touch a dividend of my superior knowledge. Some are dishonest,' and here he held up the candle, so that the light fell strongly on his visitor, 'and in that case,' he continued, 'I profit by my virtue.'

"Markheim had but just entered from the daylight streets, and his eyes had not grown familiar with the mingled shine and darkness of the shop. At these pointed words, and before the near presence of the flame, he blinked painfully and looked aside."

A little farther on:

"The dealer once more chuckled; and then, changing to his usual business voice, though still with a note of irony, 'You can give, as usual, a clear account of how you came into the possession of the object?' he continued. 'Still your uncle's cabinet? A remarkable collector, sir!'

"And the little pale, round-shouldered dealer stood almost on tiptoe, looking over the top of his gold spectacles, and nodding his head with every mark of disbelief. Markheim returned his gaze with one of infinite pity, and a touch of horror."

Note how strongly and withal how naturally the whole of this, and particularly the last sentence, suggests that Markheim has come into the shop to do murder. The story is keyed to tragedy at once, its reader with it. His mind is prepared in advance, that the significant event, when it is related, may be accepted without question.

As stated, this matter of keying the story and its reader to the pitch of the main situation or climax is not precisely the matter of atmosphere, but it has close affiliations therewith. It is even more important to the writer of fiction. Any atmospheric value in a story will be brought out by telling it justly as a course of events involving real people in a definite environment, and preparation of a reader for the main situation of a story is a part of just and adequate narration. The writer's hints of the character of what is to come must be unforced and natural, but they must be effective.

It is obvious, of course, that the more tense or strange the main situation of a story, the greater the necessity that a reader be prepared for it. If the main situation consists in commonplace characters doing some commonplace thing, a reader will accept the spectacle without artificial preparation, but if the main situation is highly dramatic, the normally placid course of a reader's thought and feeling must be agitated and stimulated in advance, or he will not rise with the climax. In other words, the fiction will not have verisimilitude emotionally. A story is both a physical spectacle and an emotional progression; the author must write both for the reader's eye and for his soul. If any story touches emotional heights, its reader must be stimulated thereto by proper preparation.

It remains to consider the matter of atmosphere, as the term is used with relation to the strict story of atmosphere, which emphasizes the emotional value of the whole for a reader rather than the significance of the events or characters.

The intrinsic difficulty to blend such diverse matters as people, events, and setting or environment into an even emotional unity requires that the strict story of atmosphere be a short story. Even if it is not a short story in point of actual length, it will be a short story in point of structure, that is, it will lead relatively few characters through little diversity of setting to a single main situation, or perhaps even to no main situation, in a dramatic sense. As noted in discussing story types, the progression of the particular atmosphere to the point of highest intensity gives the strict story of atmosphere much of its story-character. The human element is incidental and subordinate. However, the task of keeping people, events, and setting true to a fixed emotional tone is so difficult that a writer cannot sustain the effort for long. Many novels or relatively lengthy stories have high atmospheric value; Hardy's Wessex novels possess the quality, as does much of Joseph Conrad's work, "Almayer's Folly," for instance; but it is generally true that the intrinsic difficulty of the story of atmosphere tends to confine it within brief limits. It is certainly true that only the skilled hand can compass the feat of writing it at all.

I have stated that the setting of a story is not its atmosphere, and that is true. Nevertheless the setting is most often what determines the emotional effect of the whole. A hundred instances might be cited—"The Merry Men," "The Fall of the House of Usher," "Almayer's Folly," "The Return of the Native." This results from the fact that setting or environment is much more potent to produce a relatively definite emotional effect on an observer than either a person or an event, the two other elements of a story. A murder may produce a very definite feeling of horror in an observer or reader, but the emotion, while definite, is not linked inevitably to murder alone. Many other spectacles will horrify. Likewise, a person may produce a feeling of disgust in an observer or reader, but so will an infinite number of other persons, all radically different from each other and the first. But the emotional effect of the west coast of Scotland is special and peculiar to that setting; there is no single word in the language characterizing it. That is why Stevenson had to write "The Merry Men" to state it, just as Poe had to write "The Fall of the House of Usher" to state the specific emotional effect of that particular house, and Hardy had to write "The Return of the Native" to state the emotional value of his Wessex moors.

Moreover, when the writer finds the germ of his story in a person seen actually or in imagination, it is more than likely that the emphasis of the completed work will be on character, and when he finds it in an event or situation, it is more than likely that the emphasis of the completed work will be on plot. But when a countryside or house or stretch of sea-coast suggests a story, it can hardly result otherwise than that the completed work will emphasize the emotional value of the setting.

The setting of the strict story of atmosphere may determine its emotional effect, but the emotional tendency of the setting must not be affected adversely by the people or the events. That is why the setting is not atmosphere, though it may determine the atmosphere. A gloomy and terrific setting will have small emotional effect upon a reader if the people and events of the story are not such as to deepen the impression initiated by the setting, for the people and events cannot be emotionally neutral. If they are seemingly real, that is, if the story is well told apart from the matter of atmosphere, they will make some impression on a reader. Unless their impression is of a piece with that of the setting, the unity of emotional effect will be destroyed. And if there is no unity of emotional effect, there is no atmosphere, in the strict sense.

Confession is good for the soul; let me say that if there is a technique of writing so as to produce a unity of emotional effect I am unable to state it. The matter is exceptionally delicate, and only the broadest sort of abstract statement can be made. One can state—as I have stated—that the emotional effect of a story of atmosphere is usually initiated by and dependent on the setting, and that the emotional effect initiated by the setting must be reinforced by the writer's choice and handling of people and events. But that is about all that can be said. A specific story of atmosphere might be taken and examined in detail with profit, if space were available; yet the devices employed by its writer would not completely exhaust the resources of atmospheric writing, and abstract statement of them here will not cover the whole technique. Poe's technique in "The Fall of the House of Usher" is not identical with Stevenson's in "The Merry Men," nor with Conrad's in "Almayer's Folly."

Fortunately, the strict technique is not of great practical importance. Any story will gain in power by possession of an atmospheric quality, but that quality will be present if the basic conception is not trivial and feeble, and if the story is told adequately as to its three elements of setting, personality, and event. Any emotional value inherent in the thing will then be felt by a reader, as he would feel the emotional value of the spectacle, if real. Any story that is lived vicariously by its writer in the person of the character from whose viewpoint it is told, and is written justly as a course of events involving real people in a definite environment, will have all the effect on a reader attainable by the particular conception. And as to the strict story of atmosphere, it will be hopeless for the writer of fiction to attempt it until he can handle the less artificial and less difficult forms with some approach to real facility and adequacy.

One specific point of the technique of writing the strict story of atmosphere should be noted, for it is important. The emotional effect is usually initiated and determined by the setting, natural or artificial, as a tropical island or a house. Characters and events must be subservient to the particular emotional value. It results that there can be no real dramatic opposition of characters and traits in the strict story of atmosphere, for the moral nature of an individual has no affiliation with the emotional quality of a countryside or any other setting. Development of strict traits of character, which are essential to drama, will not serve to deepen for a reader the emotional suggestion of a setting. The writer of the strict story of atmosphere must seek to invest his people with such traits as will reinforce the emotional suggestion of the setting, and these traits cannot be strictly of character. Rather they will be attributes of appearance, action, mind, and soul. Insanity is an instance of such an attribute of mind, not strictly of character. The point is difficult to state abstractly, as is the whole of the technique of atmosphere, but a reading of either "The Fall of the House of Usher" or "The Merry Men" will clarify my meaning. The people of either story are less human beings than humanized emotional abstractions, of the same stuff of gloom or mystery as the house or sea. It is needless to state that the whole weakness of the story of atmosphere as a fiction results from the necessary devitalizing of its characters, for fiction primarily concerns man, his conflicts and his loves.

CHAPTER XII - THE SHORT STORY

Definition—Two Types—Dramatic Short Story—Atmospheric Short Story—Origins—Assumed Unity and Singleness of Effect of Dramatic Short Story—General Technique of Form— Characterization—Interest and Too Great Simplicity— Limitation upon Complexity—Length—Coherence of Form— Compression.

A story is a fiction with a plot, as distinguished from a tale, which is a string of incidents that happened to happen to the characters. In the story the events are linked together by the natures of the people concerned; personality influences event and event influences personality. And the short story is, simply, a short story, a fiction, possessing a plot, that could be and has been told adequately within brief limits. A plot is a dramatic problem. Therefore the short story may be defined roughly as a story embodying a dramatic problem which can be stated and worked out adequately as to all its elements of personality, event, and setting within relatively brief limits.

The general nature of the short story having been stated, it is necessary to qualify and distinguish. Fiction is concerned primarily with the intrinsic interest and significance of man and his acts, the elements of drama, but there are three fundamental types of story, two of which are normal and the other abnormal. The types are the story stressing personality and the story stressing incident, which are normal, and the story stressing atmosphere, which is abnormal in that persons and events are subordinate to the emotional value of the whole for a reader, which is usually determined by the setting. Personality is the most prominent element of the story of character, and the events are the most prominent element of the story of complication; each story stresses one of the twin elements of drama, the persons and their acts; and each story possesses both of such elements. That is, both the story of character and the strict story of plot—plot as a mere sequence of events—have some dramatic value. But the strict story of atmosphere has no dramatic value; its nature forbids that it should. The emotional effect is usually determined by the setting, and the human traits that will intensify a setting—and with which the characters must be invested—are not such as to give rise to a dramatic opposition between the persons. The definition of the short story as a story embodying a dramatic problem which can be presented adequately within brief limits does not cover the short story of atmosphere.

In other words, there are two types of short story, apart from the three types determined by the placing of emphasis upon any one of the three fictional elements of personality, event, and setting—the dramatic short story and the short story of unity of effect. The dramatic short story is either the story of character or the story of complication of incident; the short story of unity of effect is the story of atmosphere. The two types here contrasted—the dramatic story and the atmospheric story —could not be covered adequately or to any purpose by a single definition; they are radically different. In defining the short story I have defined merely the dramatic short story, and in discussing it I shall confine myself largely to the dramatic short story likewise, for the story of atmosphere has been considered elsewhere.

Knowledge of the origin of the two basic types of short story, the dramatic story and the atmospheric story, will clarify the writer's conceptions of the types. The story of atmosphere, or story of totality of emotional effect on a reader, was first consciously perfected by Poe, wherein lies America's single claim to having originated a distinct literary type. By following in prose his poetic philosophy—as stated in "The Philosophy of Composition"—Poe produced such stories as "Ligeia" and "The Fall of the House of Usher," which have little or no real dramatic value, yet which are certainly not mere tales, for they have plot- or story-value. As I have stated, in the case of the story of atmosphere, such as these two of Poe's, the climactic ascension of the particular emotional impression to the point of highest intensity supplies much of the plot-or story-element of the fiction.

On the other hand, the dramatic short story, embodying a true plot, may be said to have originated in France. The type was suggested by Poe's work; the mere mechanical hint, that of a brief story, was received eagerly by French writers, and the dramatic element, entirely altering the fundamental character of the fiction, was speedily injected. The result has been that the offshoot has entirely overshadowed the parent stem, and this simply because there is so much more material for the dramatic story than there is for the story of unity of emotional effect. The story of atmosphere is most difficult to do well, so that relatively few are published; it has no wide popular appeal, with the same result; while the range of emotional effects is narrow that may be produced on a reader by a work of fiction, that is, there is less material for the story of atmosphere than for the dramatic story.

It is time now to notice a matter concerning which much glib statement has been made, the "unity" and singleness of effect of the short story. The usual remark of the writer or talker on short story technique is that the ideal or typical short story will manifest the dramatic unities of time, place, and action, and will produce a single effect. But it is notorious that only relatively few stories do manifest the dramatic unities, so the speaker or writer goes on to say most lamely and indefinitely that the laws of technique must give way to the requirements of any particular story. Grant me for the moment that the dramatic unities are not essential to the perfect short story, that Maupassant's "The Necklace" is as technically perfect a short story as Poe's "The Cask of Amontillado," and the viciousness of preaching thus to the short story writer becomes apparent. The only definite thing he is told, that the unities are essential to the perfect short story, is false.

The vice of such statement originates in failure to distinguish between the two types of short story, the story of atmosphere and the dramatic story. The story of atmosphere, of totality or unity of emotional effect on a reader, can hardly escape manifesting the dramatic unities of place, time, and action. The emotional effect will usually be that of a single definite place, for reasons brought out in the preceding chapter; the time will be brief, on account of the inherent difficulty to sustain the atmosphere; and there will be little complication or prolongation of the action, for the same reason. But the dramatic short story is not subject to the limitations imposed by the necessity always to regard atmosphere, or emotional effect, and it may or may not manifest the dramatic unities.

The way to state the relation between the matter of unity and the dramatic short story, the short story of true plot, is this: on account of the limited space available, the plot for a dramatic short story will tend to involve relatively few shifts of setting, relatively short spaces of time, relatively few and relatively simple events, and relatively few persons. No other sort of plot can be adequately handled within narrow word limits. The short story must be written with verbal fullness and elaboration, that its phrasing may not be bare and unlike the shaded contours of life, and the plot complicated as to any one of its three elements of personality, setting, and event cannot be adequately developed in a few thousand words. The short story is the result of just conception and selection, rather than of mere rhetorical compression. Stevenson's "Markheim," for instance, is written more elaborately than almost any other episode in fiction, long or short, that is, any other episode of equal length in point of the time it would take to happen in actuality.

Poe was the first writer to say much of anything definite about his art, and commentators on technique who have followed him have merely expanded his thesis rather than said something new. The only trouble, in relation to the short story, is that Poe spoke of unity and singleness of effect with his own peculiar type of short story in mind, the short story of unity or totality of emotional effect, the short story of atmosphere. When he stated that the short story—his type of short story, the short story of atmosphere—should possess unity and produce a single effect, he stated the truth, but when it is stated that the short story meaning both the story of atmosphere and the dramatic short story—should manifest the unities and produce a single effect, the statement is false. In the first place, the dramatic short story is not the result of the same technique as the story of atmosphere; in the second place, the unity stated by Poe to be essential to the story of emotional effect is not the same thing as the old dramatic unities, which are mechanical. The fact that the story of atmosphere can hardly escape manifesting the dramatic unities does not amalgamate the two matters. Poe's unity is unity of emotional effect: the dramatic unities are singleness of time, place, and action, a matter that can be preserved by anyone, though usually at the expense of the interest of the story. How few have written and can write so as to produce a unity of emotional effect need only be suggested to enforce my point.

The matter would not be worth treating thus minutely were it not for the strong tendency to mislead of any statement that the short story must manifest the dramatic unities. Within very elastic limits, the unities are a convention of the drama, but they are not a convention of fiction, long or short. The art of the stage and the art of the story differ radically; the advantage given the play by the conciseness of its spectacle is compensated by the advantage given the story by its more inclusive character and greater flexibility. I have said that a plot or story of plot is a dramatic problem, and the word "dramatic" has connotations of the stage, but what was meant was that a plot is a conflict between persons, within a single person, or with nature. It was not meant that a plot or story of plot is subject to the conventions of the stage. The art of fiction is infinitely more inclusive and flexible than the art of the stage, and the writer of fiction must utilize to the full the advantages of his art in order to compensate his work in the eyes of a reader for its weakness—relative to the play—in vividness and body.

One may say that the spectacle of life is infinitely various, so that the writer of fiction has plenty of material for stories at hand. But life, despite the efforts of Mrs. Grundy, is subject to no conventions, social, moral, or artistic, and the short story writer who brings all his ideas to the dramatic unities as a first test will winnow little grain from the chaff. When the short story writer finds a hint for a story he should consider whether he can bring out with his few thousand words all the matters necessary to the fiction's having full effect on a reader, but the less he frets about any abstract unity or singleness of effect the better. The words have a plausible sound in discussion, but they mean nothing, except in relation to the story of atmosphere. It means something to say that the dramatic short story should possess unity of tone; it means something to say that it should possess unity of style; but it means nothing to say that it should possess unity, simply, unless the dramatic unities are meant, and in that case the statement is false. Some short stories happen to possess the dramatic unities; more do not.

By the very nature of the conceptive process the writer seizes his story ideas in terms of persons, events, or atmosphere. And when he has a definite story idea he first should develop it so as to give it maximum effect, and then should consider whether he must write a short story or novel or romance to give his developed idea adequate expression. The writer who starts with some abstract knowledge of fiction technique, and seeks to vivify rules of construction into a definite story, will accomplish very little. Good stories are not conceived that way, and good writers do not go to work that way. The story is the thing, and it does not lie between the covers of this or any other book on technique. It lies in the people and events the writer sees in reality or in imagination, and to find it the writer must turn to life or to his dreams. After the story is found the writer's knowledge of and facility in technique will come into play in the work of development and execution.

The broad outlines of the technique of the dramatic short story were implied in the statement that it will tend to involve relatively few shifts of setting, relatively short spaces of time, relatively few and relatively simple events, and relatively few persons. Its unity of tone—which is characteristic of the short story, dramatic and of atmosphere—results from its simplicity as to persons, events, and setting, and its unity of style results from its unity of tone. The elements of the short story are less complex than those of a longer fiction, and the fact causes all the modifications in the general technique of fiction as manifested by the short story. In the short story, for instance, there is less opportunity than in the novel to manage secondary events to build up character or personality. The whole process must be swifter, and the writer must depend largely on direct statement and description.

This matter is of some importance. As to setting, the technique of the short story and of the novel are identical; there is merely less setting in the short story—speaking quantitatively— because the type involves fewer shifts of place, even if the action does not happen in one place. And the technique of the short story and of the novel are identical as to action; the short story merely involves fewer episodes. But as to the people, the technique of the short story and of the novel differ. It is true that the short story involves few persons, relatively to the novel, just as it involves relatively few shifts of setting and relatively few events, but the difference is more than quantitative, and so affects the technique of the type. It affects the technique of the short story because characterization is a matter achieved by showing the person in action, by describing him, by transcribing his speech, and by stating his qualities directly. That is to say, characterization goes on in every part of the story, except where setting is being touched in. And it will go on there, to a slight extent, if the environment is given in terms of the impressions received by the character affected. On the other hand, narration, or verbal treatment of the event, and the description of setting, or verbal treatment of the environment, are more or less distinct and separate elements of a story. The matter is delicate, and I run some risk of being obscure here, but the net result of the simplicity and separateness of both the narrative and the descriptive process is that the narrative and descriptive technique of the short story is the narrative and descriptive technique of fiction generally. Writer of novel and writer of short story can narrate a murder in much the same way, or touch in a countryside with identical technique, but they cannot handle their people similarly.

Perhaps the point can be made clearer. The writer of a novel and the writer of a short story alike must invest their people with the vivacity, distinction, and concreteness of real men and women, but where the one has five hundred pages, let us say, the other has only five thousand words. It is a task difficult enough at best to precipitate a man in a few drops of ink. It is also difficult to narrate the man's actions with some of the vividness of reality, or to touch in a real world for him to move in. But note this. Where the novelist must deal with a large number of events and scenes, the short story writer has only a few to handle; he has about as many words available for each of his few as the novelist has for his many. That is not the case in creating characters. The process of characterization must permeate any fiction, forwarded by the narrative matter, the dialogue, the expository matter, and the descriptive matter alike. And the novelist has five hundred pages to initiate, reinforce, and complete the illusion of personality where the short story writer has but five thousand words. The novelist has more people to vivify, it is true, but not enough more than the short story writer to give the latter an equal chance if he follows the same technique.

It all comes down to this: a story, long or short, can be broken up into its several episodes and scenes, which are mechanically separable, but its people move through the whole. Since any event or any scene is in a sense a mere item of a story, not universally influential, the technique of handling event or scene simply as such is much the same, whatever the type of story. But since the element of personality is universally present and influential in a story, the technique of characterization varies with the essential nature of the story as a whole.

The result of the condition upon the general technique of characterization as applied in the short story must now be stated.

I have said already that the whole process must be swifter, but that is not very definite. Expanded, the statement amounts to saying that the short story writer cannot develop personality with the fullness and diversity of the novelist; he must concentrate his verbal resources upon the trait developed by the few events of the story and upon a few striking peculiarities of appearance and speech. As to the strict trait of character, the story itself will point the way. It will have one main situation, and probably that one will be of such a nature as to involve relatively simple attributes of soul in the persons concerned. As to the more superficial matter of making the persons seem real and lifelike, the writer must describe sharply, rather than at length—as Stevenson did in "A Lodging for the Night"—and must make his people talk as individually as possible. The general aim, of course, is the same as in the longer story, to present real characters of unique appearance and speech. And the writer's resources—again of course—are the same, but the brevity of the short story forces him to concentrate upon one matter of soul, one matter—or at most a few—of appearance, and one matter of speech. The whole art of fiction is selective; even the novel cannot present justly the complete man; and the short story, simply because it is short, is the most highly selective fiction of all. It cannot present the whole man, but it must seem to. A reader will not feel the absence of traits not involved in the events, and by vivid and brief descriptive touches, reinforced by unique speech, any character can be invested with what will be accepted as a complete physical presence.

As stated, the story itself, if a true story and not a tale, will show its writer that his expository matter or direct statement as to character must bear only upon the traits involved in the plot-situation of the story. The necessity is not peculiar to the short story, but it is more insistent than in the case of the novel. The other points of the technique of characterizing in the short story are purely verbal, and the writer's success depends upon his faculty in pungent description and in handling speech.

The remainder of the technique of the short story, apart from the matter of creating real men and women, is not verbal, but constructive, and is implied in—as it results from—the brevity of the fiction. Unlike the novelist, the writer of the short story has space for nothing but the story. He cannot drag in by the heels episodes unessential to the story solely for the sake of their intrinsic interest; he cannot waste words upon unessential persons. He is faced by two facts—that his story must be interesting, so that it will probably have to involve considerable complication as to persons, events, and setting, and that it must be told with enough verbal fullness and elaboration to give it the body and seeming of life. Trimming between the necessity to interest and the necessity to invest his story with reality, the writer first must find an interesting story, and then, in writing, or in developing and writing, must be vigilant to transcribe nothing unessential to the story, or he will be forced to exceed his space-limit.

The process comprehends most of the technique of the short story. The whole difference between it and the novel is that the novel is more discursive. Much of the novel's interest, quite permissibly, may inhere in persons, episodes, and matter generally without relation to the main thread of the story. But a short story's interest may not inhere in matter foreign to the thread of the story. That is the case not because of any arbitrary requirement that it be a "unity," but simply because a short story cannot be told adequately as to the story without exceeding the word-limit if unessential matter be incorporated with it.

The fallacy, whether on the part of commentator on technique or writer of fiction, in approaching the short story as some sort of artificial fictional unity lies in the implicit disregard of the necessity to interest. The first necessity is that a story interest, and to meet it the writer must devise some complication of persons, motives, and events, and usually that will involve some diversity of setting, or change of place. The second necessity is that the story be told so as to create the illusion of reality, and to meet it the writer will be forced to exhaust his few thousand words. The necessity that the story interest can be met only rarely without violating the unities of the drama; therefore they are not a convention of the art of the short story. Apart from the matter of unity of tone and style, the short story is a unity only in that it is one single story, nothing more, nothing less. That is, each word is essential to the fiction as such. But that does not mean that the story or plot is a unity in itself. It may involve much diversity in the three fictional elements of personality, event, and setting, the last of which includes time.

I emphasize the matter because the beginning writer is apt to devise stories too simple to present a real problem to awaken a reader's interest. There is also the converse fault, of course, that of devising a story too complicated to be given adequate expression in few words, but this fault will tend to correct itself through the difficulties the writer will meet in execution. The other will not tend to correct itself. The more simple the story, the easier it will be to write with some approach to adequacy. The writer who fancies that a short story must involve as little as possible diversity of people, events, and places may very well continue to devise stories too simple to awaken interest, however effectively they may be told. He will have no trouble in writing each one within his space, but he will have trouble in getting them published, for each will be lacking in essential fictional value, the capacity to interest. Here I can make only general statement, and it is impracticable to dwell on the fact

that real and highly individualized characters will invest a
simple story with all the interest of a more complicated fiction.
The general truth, however, is that the interest of a tale lies in
the problem it presents and solves, that a problem involves
complication and diversity, and that a writer may go astray who
seeks only the dramatically unified and simple plot. His work
will interest a reader if he creates real people, but the capacity
to do so is a rare faculty. At the bottom of it, a story, long or
short, is a sequence of events; they should not be too simple,
for, apart from the human element, simplicity presents no
problem to awaken a reader's interest.

The sole limitation upon the complexity and diversity of the
short story as a whole is the difficulty to develop in few words a
plot complicated as to personality, event, place, or time.
Accordingly, the plot suitable for a short story will tend to be
simple, but it need not be so simple that the events, apart from
the people, will not awaken interest. Moreover, the unskilled
writer who has experienced the difficulty to develop an
interesting plot in few words will be astonished by the results of
a little forethought and careful planning before writing.
Elimination and suppression of inessential and relatively
unimportant matters will enable him to set forth adequately,
though in a few words, a story of real body and interest.

The whole discussion should awaken realization of the fact that
the short story is the most difficult form of prose fiction. To the
general difficulty of all fiction it adds the difficulty that
whatever is done must be done in a few words. The writer of
novel or romance has only to interest, and his space is
practically unlimited. The short story writer must interest, and
he must interest in few words and pages. He must depend
solely on his story; he has space for nothing else. He should
remember that each item of unessential matter given place by
him will lessen by just so much the number of words available
to give the real story verisimilitude and consequent interest
and appeal. To take the conceptive aspect of it, in devising a
short story he should remember that inclusion of any
accidental and unessential matter must lessen by just so much
his power to awaken interest by some diversity and
complication in the real story.

When a story idea is found, the writer should determine precisely what matters must be brought out if the fiction is to have full effect on a reader, who will have only the writer's words to go on. The writer should realize precisely what elements of personality are significant in relation to the main situation, which is the story in little, and should prepare to develop the motives and traits involved. He should determine precisely what will be the most effective physical movement for the story, the nature and order of events, also the setting or environment. He should consider the essential nature of the main situation, or climax, and, if he cannot manage that preceding events shall prepare a reader for it, he should prepare from the beginning of the story to hint what is to come, as Stevenson does in "Markheim." Finally, he should grasp the developed story as a whole, and be vigilant to transcribe nothing unessential, for if the story is real fictional knot or problem, and worth while, he cannot do so without sacrificing essential matter or exceeding his limits.

The physical brevity of the short story certainly has great influence in the direction of simplicity. But its brevity does not subject the dramatic short story to the conventions of the stage. It must be a unity, so-called, but only in this, that every word must be necessary to develop the story-idea, which, in itself, may be simple or somewhat complex. The short story of atmosphere is another matter.

Coherence is a word much better than unity to express the most significant attribute of the dramatic short story. The form is coherent in that every word, line, and sentence has relation to the story itself. The novel is relatively incoherent in that it often embodies whole stories without relation to the main story, or matter without relation to any story at all. The most pungent way to put the point of the whole discussion is to state that the short story, viewed merely as a sequence of words, is coherent in that each word serves to forward a single story-idea to its conclusion. That is not to state that the story-idea itself is coherent or a unity. It is a unity in that it is single, one story, but the one story need not manifest unity of time, place, and action. The sooner the short story writer clears his head of any notion that the verbal coherence of the dramatic short story involves some indefinable unity in its matter or story-idea, or some equally indefinable singleness of effect, the better for him, his work and pocketbook.[Q]

There would be no great profit in summarizing here the items of technique treated in other chapters. All are of use in the short story, functioning as in other forms of prose fiction. Apart from the matter of characterization, the peculiar technique of the short story is constructive and supervisory, rather than executive. The writer must make certain that he has one story and nothing else, for only one story can be adequately developed within brief limits. In writing, he must take care to transcribe only story-matter, for the same reason. But in narrating an event, or in describing a setting, after he has determined that event and setting are essential to his single story, the writer may employ the technique of general narrative or descriptive writing. Whatever the form of fiction, its aim is the same, to show real men and women doing in a real world the things one might expect from their natures and the circumstances of their lives.

In the chapter on story types something was said as to the current insistence upon the verbal compression of the short story. As stated there, the short story, dramatic or atmospheric, is not the result of mere rhetorical compression, rather of the inherent brevity of the conception. The executive technique of long story and short are identical, except as to the single matter of characterization. The short story develops its fewer episodes with as much rhetorical elaboration as the novel develops its many, and the writer who conceives that a short story can be produced by verbal paring and filing is on the highroad to failure.

CHAPTER XIII - THE NOVEL

Novel and Romance—Romanticism and Realism—Techniques of Novel and Romance—Incoherence of Novel Relative to Short Story—Novel as Medium of Self-Expression— Interpolation of Personal Comment—Significant Simplicity— Permissible Inclusiveness of Novel—Full Development of Personality—Variety of Action—Length—Initial Idea—Story— Life—Society—Singleness of Story—Social Emphasis.

I have a small dictionary on my desk which defines the novel as a "fictitious prose narrative or tale presenting a picture of real life," and the romance as "any fictitious and wonderful tale: a fictitious narrative in prose or verse which passes beyond the limits of real life." The definitions state a distinction easier to feel vaguely than to justify. One may say with truth that Jane Austen's "Sense and Sensibility" or Trollope's "The Warden" presents a picture of real life, but can one also say with truth that Hawthorne's "The Scarlet Letter" or Stevenson's "Dr. Jekyll and Mr. Hyde" passes essentially beyond the limits of real life simply because each book states a physically impossible thing—the brand of his sin over Arthur Dimmesdale's heart and the metamorphosis of Dr. Jekyll? Either matter is a mere symbol, devised to give concreteness to a spiritual fact. Is it not true than human life, the material for fiction, has its spiritual actualities as well as its physical facts? and does not the romance—as it is commonly understood— differ from the novel merely in that it narrates a real adventure of the soul rather than a real adventure of the body?

The fact is patent, I think, that the writer of fiction will gain small benefit from conceiving the romance as something separate and apart from the novel; likewise, that a book on technique without confusion may treat the writing of long fiction generally as the writing of novels. It is true, of course, that the essential bent of any particular writer may lead him to deal with the facts of the soul rather than the facts of the body, or that any particular story may be a spiritual rather than a physical adventure; nevertheless the story of the spirit must still develop facts and show their relations, and the technical resources of its writer are precisely the same as those of the writer who deals predominately with the more concrete physical facts of life.

It would be interesting to go at some length into this question of romance, all its connotations and implications. In particular, there is an antithesis in common thought, with romanticism and realism the two opposed members, which it would not be too dull to discuss. But the discussion would not give much light to one who desires to acquire a knowledge of the mechanics of fiction, long or short. It is permissible to call a realist one who transcribes predominately physical details, and it is permissible to call a romanticist one who transcribes predominated [typo for "predominantly"?] spiritual details, but in both cases the basic technique is identical. The realist can confine himself to physical facts because his story deals largely with the everyday actualities of life, and its subordinate spiritual values will be felt by a reader through inference from the facts. The romanticist must state spiritual facts directly because they are the very stuff and essence of his story. He is none the less a realist if there are spiritual actualities—an indisputable proposition—and if he states them as they exist for him.

The critical discussion that treats realism and romanticism as opposed artistic philosophies is so confused that it would serve no useful purpose to go into the matter here. What little I have to say on the subject will be said in the next chapter. But it is not inappropriate to call attention to the fact that every story conceived—in Stevenson's phrase—from within outwards, the only genesis for a work of art, is merely a subjective reality; it never happened. Perhaps it is so essentially commonplace that it probably has happened sometime; perhaps it is so little abnormal that very possibly it has happened. Or perhaps it may be of such a nature that it never could have happened. In any event, whatever the nature of the story, its verity and reality as a fiction depend solely upon its writer's elaborative and executive powers. If his hand falter, tangibility and concreteness in the matter of the story will not save it, will not make it seem real to a reader. The lives of most men are commonplace, but the relatively few lives that are not commonplace are as real and actual as those that follow beaten paths. In the lives of most, the spiritual element is subordinate, perhaps, but in the lives of some few it is enormously influential and supremely real. Realism, the artistic philosophy, asserts that fiction should present only the real. The assertion is nonsense for two reasons. First, the commonplace, or, if you please the inevitable, the only reality which realism admits, is not the only reality. Second, the verity or reality of fiction cannot be ascertained by any objective test, cannot be determined by the physical possibility of its matter, its people and their acts, for a fiction is purely subjective, a conception, and conceivability is the sole test of its verity. The writer of a story transcribes what he sees, not necessarily what is.[R]

As stated, the writer of fiction will derive small benefit from conceiving novel and romance as entirely different types of fiction. The distinction between them used to be insisted upon much more pedantically than is the case to-day, and the present tendency to call any story of book-length a novel is a healthy sign. The technique of the novel, in the narrow sense of a picture of society, and the technique of the romance, in the narrow sense of a story not of "real" life, are broadly the same. And where there is no difference in technique the artist should admit no difference in type. If he does admit any difference in type, and allows it to influence him, his conceptive faculty will be hampered and that is artistic death. It is hard enough to find a story that is worth while, a story that will interest, without subjecting one's self to the added and totally unnecessary difficulty to bring all one's ideas to the measure of some fancied type as a first test. The writer of fiction should be warned that it is supremely difficult to avoid becoming artificial and mechanical, and that he will surely become so if he does his conceptive thinking in terms of analysis. In the first place, the analytical habit of mind is directly opposed to the creative; in the second place, the analysis that divides long stories into novels and romances in the special sense is false. The way to find a story is to look for a story, forgetting all that pedants have written and failures practiced. The silly criticism that classifies fiction by its content is beneath contempt; the writer of fiction who heeds it is supremely foolish.

In the following discussion the term "novel" will be used simply to denote a plotted fiction of book-length.

Contrasting the short story and the novel, and dwelling on the relative coherence of the briefer form, I had occasion to state that the novel is relatively incoherent in that much of its interest for a reader quite permissibly may inhere in matter with little or no relation to the main thread of the story. Of course, incoherence is not a point of the technique of the novel. Incoherence is not a point of the technique of anything, except of some of the ultra modern schools in music, painting, and verse. The statement as to the incoherence of the novel was made incidentally in developing the argument that the short story cannot be incoherent because its brevity forbids that it present even its single story-idea adequately and also set forth irrelevant matter. On the other hand, the novel may set forth irrelevant matter because its length is not only a greater but a more elastic quantity than that of the short story; if the interruptions of the story are not too frequent and sustained, the power of the story over a reader will not be lessened to any appreciable extent. That is not to say that the novelist should seek to interrupt himself.

A good many serious writers—so-called—choose to write the novel simply because it does offer an opportunity for direct self-expression greater than any afforded by briefer fiction. They are confined to fiction—may they pardon the remark— because they have met, or feel that they will meet, difficulty in finding a publisher for their various theories stated as such; so they blithely write a novel, with insertions of politics, religion, sociology, what not, and palm it off on the unhappy public for a story. Of course such direct expression of one's opinions is not self-expression through the medium of a work of art. It is only choosing deliberately to do poor work for the sake of money or notoriety or vanity. Writing the "problem novel" is not quite the same thing. If a social problem, as the friction between capital and labor, is utilized as the fundamental plot—or conflict- theme of a novel, a good deal of personal opinion may be introduced by the author without injury to the artistic coherence of the story. But it is well to remember that the primary aim of fiction is to interest, an aim that can be achieved most easily and most completely by telling a good story. Propaganda is apt to be supremely dull anyway, and it is bound to seem dull to one who is looking for a story and nothing else. The practical implications of a work of art must be mere implications, resting in inference, or the work will be feeble and misshapen.

The novelist can indulge in personal comment and yet present the whole of his story, for his space is practically unlimited. The writer of the short story must sacrifice either the comment or the story. The result is that the typical novel is more incoherent than the typical short story. The finer the book as a whole, the easier it is to forgive or overlook the defect, for defect it is. One can forgive Thackeray his rambling asides and his diffidence in approaching his story, for in all of his books the story is present and in each it is a fine thing. But "Vanity Fair," for instance, is too significant a fiction to suffer constant interruption without causing a reader to become impatient. If a story is essentially weak, interpolating personal comment and unrelated matter generally will make it weaker; if it is essentially fine and significant, passages without bearing on the story will irritate the reader.

Whatever the art, whoever the artist, his task is to hold pen or chisel or brush true to the outlines of his conception. If his hand leave its proper course, whether of set purpose or through inaptitude, his work must suffer. The art of fiction is so infinitely difficult that the practitioner should welcome rather than bewail his obligation to hew to the line, for by concentrating upon the story and nothing else he will be led to leave no gaps in his presentment. A work of art is a thing of significant simplicity. Just because the novelist works in words, just because his materials have some significance for a reader in themselves—unlike the clay and marble of the sculptor, the stone of the architect, and the pigments of the painter, which, unwrought upon, have no message for an observer—the novelist is not at liberty to throw words together without some set purpose. The inherent significance of each word must have just relation to the whole, if the whole is to have the direction and significant simplicity of a work of art. The real condition is that the novelist, unlike the writer of the short story, may tell his story adequately and do something else, but the artistic quality of his work will suffer, that is, its power over a reader will be diminished, if he interpolates foreign matter. Artistry is simply the faculty to realize to the utmost the inherent power of one's conceptions, and the artistry of any fiction lessens as the appeal of the story for a reader diminishes. And the appeal of a story as such must diminish with every interruption, unless its power over a reader be very great, and in that case any break in its movement will irritate and offend.

I have cited Stevenson's "The Ebb-Tide" a number of times already, and the book may be instanced here. It is a tremendously powerful bit of work, considering the nature of its matter, and its power over a reader in large part results from its author's having confined himself strictly to the story. The conception is significant, and the story as written is significant because the conception is set forth whole and unmarred. The reader's attention is not distracted by matter irrelevant to the story. Its theme, the impossibility that a weak man should be other than weak, however he may be circumstanced, is developed adequately, and nothing else is developed. No book could be more wisely recommended to the writer of fiction for study of the essential technical processes of fiction. It shows adequate treatment of personality, adequate treatment of events, and adequate treatment of setting, shows fictionally real people doing fictionally real things in a fictionally real environment. Above all, it is a story, nothing else, and is pointed to bring out its value as a whole; that is it has the significant simplicity of a true work of art. It is coherent as to the story it embodies, and in its coherence lies its power. The bare conception is somewhat weak in that it tends to arouse an intellectual rather than an emotional interest in a reader; moreover, the conception is positively unpleasant and depressing, in the conventional sense; but the book as written is a powerful thing because it realizes to the full the inherent capacity of its matter to interest and impress by telling the story adequately and by bringing out nothing but the story.[S]

The novel, then, should be coherent as to the story it embodies, but that is not the whole of its peculiar technique. The story itself may be widely inclusive, may, in a way, involve a number of stories. The novelist should not seek deliberately to combine the unrelated, but he need not follow a single thread. He can turn aside into bypaths of action that will bring out the natures of his people with more fullness than the straight course of the story itself, and he can involve his minor characters in sub-plots, relatively unimportant stories of their own. Generally, the novelist will seek to develop personality with greater fullness and detail than the writer of the short story, and, as a result, the action of the novel will be more diffused and looser, less pointed, than the action of the short story. Or, conversely, the long story necessarily involves more varied action than the briefer form, and therefore develops more varied traits in the actors. Relative to the short story, the novel is a natural type of fiction in that it can make some approach to presenting the whole man, with all his contradictory and inconsistent traits and impulses; relative to the novel, the short story is an artificial type of fiction in that the comparatively direct and pointed character of its action forbids that it develop more than one or a few significant traits of personality. The writer of the short story cannot qualify and distinguish as to his people's natures, and that is why the fine short story is less humanly significant than the fine novel, for no man is pure saint or pure villain, pure this or pure that. We are all bewilderingly inconsistent, wherein lies most of the interest of life. The novel can show its people blown here and there by the winds of desire, as in life, and that is what the short story cannot do.

Each story is a rule to itself, so far as the question of scope and variety of action is concerned, but the novelist will derive small benefit from introducing unnecessary people and unnecessary events merely to lend a greater illusion of movement or bustle to the whole. Action, in fiction, is action which plays a necessary part in the story, and the novelist should not interpolate insignificant events any more than he should interpolate his own opinions on life and morals. His task is to tell some particular story, no more, no less.

It is difficult to state the relative inclusiveness of the novel without laying a false emphasis on its permissible scope and variety of content, for the novel should be exclusive as well as inclusive. That is, it should not be a mere welter of people and what they do, but should possess some single human significance, some primary reason for being, by which its writer can test the availability of matter that suggests itself to him. Between the conciseness and singleness of "The Ebb-Tide" and the unnecessary length and complexity of some of the Victorians lies a golden mean easier to recognize in specific books than to state abstractedly. "The Ebb-Tide," though not a short story in point of length, is somewhat brief, and it is a short story in structure, in point of the singleness of its story-idea, the small number of its characters, and the comparative simplicity of its action. Of course, it is none the less a fine novel, a fine long story; the point is that there are thousands of other stories, equally fine, perhaps more humanly significant, which cannot be written so concisely, but which need not run to the length of "David Copperfield," "The Virginians," or "The Cloister and the Hearth." To attempt to set mechanical limits of length for the novel would be mere silliness, but it is true that the average idea for a long story can be given complete and adequate expression in one or two hundred thousand words. Usually there is no need to write at much greater or inordinate length, unless irrelevant matter is introduced for its own sake. And the introduction of such matter for its own sake can only hinder the effect of the story itself on a reader. It may render the book, the mere sequence of words, more interesting, but irrelevant matter cannot render the story itself more interesting. The distinction should be noted and realized, for the novelist's aim is to interest through his story, not merely to interest.

There is another way to approach the matter of the novel's relative inclusiveness and length, perhaps a better way. Where the novelist first conceives his story definitely as such, as a course of events, he should bring all matter which suggests itself for writing to the test of relation to the story. He has only to write the story, duly elaborated, and thereby he will take care of the matters of length and complexity and inclusiveness without detached calculation to that end. But if the novelist finds his initial idea in terms of a life or of a phase of society, the idea does not plot or diagram the whole story for him. He has yet to evolve the story as such, and he may devise as short and simple a thing as "The Ebb-Tide" or as long and complicated a thing as Tolstoi's "War and Peace." Usually it will be found, I think, that the very long novel—"Tom Jones," "Jean Christophe," "David Copperfield," "Anna Karenina," "Les Miserables," "The Virginians"—was first conceived in terms of a life or a society, rather than in terms of a definite story. It is certainly true that only the life of an individual or the life of a society can serve to bind together the motley elements of a very long novel, giving it some artistic coherence. "David Copperfield" can be called one story in that it consists of Copperfield's life and related matters, but "Our Mutual Friend" is in no sense a single story. It is merely a number of stories devised to be told together and therefore dovetailing to some extent.

It all comes down to this: if the novelist conceives a definite story, he has only to tell it, but if he conceives a life or a society he has yet to devise his story. And the matters which can have some relation to a life or a society are much more varied than those which can have some relation to a course of events. In other words, the conception of a story as such limits the writer's choice of matter. If one starts with a story, one can tell only the story. If one starts with a life or a society, one can write pretty much at large.

In discussing the short story, it was possible to state that it must embody one story-idea, for the physical brevity of the form prohibits adequate development of more than a single story. But if I stated that the novel must embody one story-idea, no more, no less, the statement would be false, for the length of the form is practically unlimited. As Dickens did in "Our Mutual Friend" and other books, the novelist can tell together three or four unrelated stories if he so desires. He has the space. The question is not whether he can but whether he should tell more than one. The answer is that he should confine himself to one. Perhaps a little supporting argument is called for.

The most obvious criticism of this limitation upon the novelist is that it savors strongly of artificiality, rather than of art. The reader may think of Dickens himself, his marvelous people, the world of delight in his books. But Dickens, it may be said with all reverence, was no story-teller. His is a fictional world turned upside down. His stories are less than nothing; his major characters are less than nothing; but his little people are gods. All his books are mere cardboard beside the works of such a one as Dostoievsky, but in each book—with a few exceptions— there is some stupendous Weller or Micawber, not a man, but a god. One goes to Dickens almost as to vaudeville, and "Pickwick" is his best book because it is no story. In it Weller and the others run wild unrestrained by the necessities of any predetermined course of events. But a story is a predetermined course of events, actually or in effect, and the mere fact that Dickens could write poor stories and yet interest by his wonderful people does not falsify the technique of fiction.

Again, the fact that the novelist should confine himself to one story at a time does not debar him from following side-issues, provided they have relation to the main course of events, or from creating minor people like Dickens', if he has the power. Dickens could have placed his people in real stories instead of in the weak fictions they serve to ennoble.

Finally, I will state abstractly the conditions from which result the artistic, not the physical necessity that the novelist confine himself in each book to a single story-idea.

The aim to interest is the aim of fiction, long and short, and the body of a writer's resources to accomplish the aim make up the body of fiction technique. But the aim of the writer of plotted fiction is not simply to interest; it is to interest through a story, a course of events functioning together in that they embody some sort of problem. Leaving aside the matter of executive artistry, and premising that the writer will realize to the full the possibilities of his story, it is accurate to state that the interest a story will arouse will be in accordance with the human significance of the problem it embodies. Adequate fictional treatment of the problem to win love or to make a living will be more interesting than adequate fictional treatment of the problem to escape payment of an income tax. And the possibilities of any problem of life to arouse a reader's interest can be realized to the full only by setting out that problem and nothing else. Only by showing the thing in isolation and high relief can the writer reveal to, and force home upon a reader its ultimate significance. If anything unrelated to the story or problem is brought out, something of the power of the story as such will be lost. Likewise, if two or more stories or problems are each completely developed in one book, neither will have that singleness of appeal to a reader which is essential if each is to have maximum effect.

In other words, a novel does not function as a mere physical spectacle; being a story, it must have a motive, an artistic purpose; and if it has more than one it will be at cross purposes as a work of art. That is not a mere "artistic" defect. It is a practical defect in that motive, purpose, and story will not have extreme effect. Nor is it to say that the novel may not be very complicated as to any or all of its three elements of people, events, and setting. "Anna Karenina" is complicated enough, in all conscience, but every item of the novel has relation to its one story either in that it serves directly to develop the horrible tragedy of Anna's life or in that it forwards the presentment of the society which she renounced.

The painter cannot put two different pictures side by side on the same canvas without hampering the effect of each; still less can he commingle the two. The architect cannot build on two designs at once. Nor can the novelist—if he would have each story realize to the full its inherent capacity to interest— combine different stories in the same book. He can develop personality in great detail; he can follow by-paths of action; he can involve his minor characters in subplots; but the main course of the story must be single, not duplicate or triplicate, that the whole may have point and significance.

The reader will observe that this book lays absolutely no restrictions on the conceptive faculty. It preaches that the way to write fiction is to look for a story, and, when it is found, to write it so as to give it full effect. It may be a short story; it may be a novel. It may have its genesis in a dream, in a life, in a situation, in a society. But, whatever its nature, whatever its length, its effect on, its interest for, a reader, can result only from itself. The story as such cannot be fortified by the introduction of foreign matter, although the interest of the writer's text as a mere sequence of words may be heightened thereby. But the aim of the writer of novel or short story is to interest through his story as such, not merely to interest. A newspaper is interesting, yet a newspaper is not a story, however much fiction it may embody.

The novel or long story is apt to have a strong social emphasis simply because the interplay of society and the conflict of its members supply much more material for stories than the more isolated phases of human life. The novelist is under no obligation to reproduce a social spectacle in each book, but more often than not he will find that he must do so to bring out the full value of his conception. It follows that he will do well to go about with an observant eye, for it is the little details of the novel of manners that lend verisimilitude to the whole. And such matters cannot be invented; they must have been observed; for a reader knows them whether or not the writer does too.

CHAPTER XIV - CONCLUSION

Story and Tale—Realism the Method—Realism the Dogma—
Philosophy of Fiction—Interest—Power of the Real Problems
of Life—Test of Merit—Aim of Executive Artistry—
Verisimilitude—Ultimate Artistic Significance of Plot.

The purpose of this book has been to shed a little light on the
essential technical processes of the art of fiction; to state a
general philosophy of fiction has not been my aim. Accordingly,
the text touches only incidentally upon the fundamental types
of fiction and a writer's fundamental purposes in adopting any
one of them as a medium for expression of himself or his
conceptions. Partly to justify some of the text, and partly
because it may prove of practical service, I shall state briefly a
general theory or philosophy of fiction-not my theory, merely,
nor that of anyone else, but simply the theory which is implied
in the content and aim of the art itself.

The content of fiction is man and what he may experience, in
body, mind, and soul; the aim of fiction is to interest. Certain
results follow, but before stating them it will be well to clear the
way a little.

I have stated that a story is a fiction with a plot, and have
defined a plot as a dramatic problem, that is, a course of events
which function together as a whole in that they influence and
are influenced by character or personality. And nine-tenths of
the technique of fiction is concerned with the object to develop
a plot. To develop a tale, a fiction, long or short, without a plot,
only direct narrative and descriptive writing is requisite; it is
the plot-element of a fiction, with all its implications as to
personality, that forces the writer of a story—a fiction with a
plot—to weave together cunningly each strand of his matter,
narrative, exposition, dialogue, description, that the whole
pattern may show fictionally real people doing in a fictionally
real world what one might naturally expect from their natures
and the circumstances of their lives. The task is infinitely more
difficult and delicate than to take a Sinbad the Sailor or a
Cinderella through a course of happenings without essential
relation to the nature of either person, who is, in each case, a
mere human focal point for the events to be precipitated upon.

Accordingly, this book concentrates upon the fiction of plot, or story, rather than the fiction without plot, or tale. The technique of the fiction of plot comprehends and includes the technique of the tale, which could be ignored here without loss.

Whether or not a fiction possess a plot, and is a story, or lacks a plot, and is a tale, it will be concerned with people and what they do, the man and his acts. Long or short, a fiction must deal with man, at least with personality, as do London's "The Call of the Wild" and Kipling's "The Ship That Found Herself." Since fiction deals with man, it deals both with physical and spiritual facts, with the facts of the soul and the more tangible things of the body and the earth. It results that either the spiritual or physical element of any fiction may largely outweigh the other, at least, preponderate over it. That is, the long story may be what is known as a novel or what is known as a romance, and the brief story may reveal the fate of the spirit rather than the fate of the body and mind.[T]

Precisely at this point one encounters a difficulty raised by critical comment on fiction, the whole complex of obscurantism about "realism" and "romanticism." Instead of wasting space in trying to unravel the threads of the tangle as stated by those who have knotted it, it will be much easier and much more profitable to state a few facts that will demonstrate the essential fallacy of such discussion.

In the first place, realism characterizes a method, one that might better be called the method of stating the concrete in detail. If a story is concerned largely with the more common actualities of everyday life, it is possible that its writer may best create his illusion of reality by itemizing the physical facts in some detail.

In the second place, "realism" has been elevated from a mere technical method into an artistic creed or dogma. The assumption is made that only the more tangible matters of life are realities, and that fiction should seek to present only the real.

It is unnecessary to do more than state that the first term of this assumption is false. Not only are there facts of the spirit as well as facts of the body and the phenomenal universe, but the spiritual fact is precisely the fact which is fictionally significant. Fiction deals with man for man, and man is man just and only because he has an intelligence and a soul, enabling him to impose his will upon brute matter and to rise superior to evil fortune.

The second term of the realists' assumption is that fiction should present only the real. And the essential fallacy of the assumption is this: it ignores the fact that the first aim of fiction is to interest. Philosophy, not fiction, must give us a test of truth and reality. Irrespective of what is real—a question that the confirmed realist answers falsely, because partially and exclusively—one who denies the reality and significance of the spiritual life of man, and therefore refuses to give it fictional treatment, debars himself from presenting much interesting matter.

It might not be too dull, incidentally, to go into the question of how much the world of the spirit shall be allowed to impose its necessities on the world of the flesh, but the matter is subordinate, part of the general question of verisimilitude. Frequently, to give concrete fictional treatment to a fact of the soul, the writer will have to falsify deliberately as to physical facts, as Stevenson did in "Dr. Jekyll and Mr. Hyde."

Realism, the technical method expanded into an artistic dogma, has much to answer for. In the hands of the French, it has been responsible for much that is uselessly unpleasant and brutal; in the hands of English and American writers, it has been responsible for much dullness. The unpleasant facts and petty concerns of life alike are significant only in relation to the persons they affect; in themselves, they are dreary or repellent items. If the ugly fact has no relation to the story as such, it should not be given place; if the commonplace detail has no relation to the course of the story, and will perform no office in lending reality to the fiction in a reader's eyes, it should not be transcribed.

The misconceptions that cluster about realism the dogma affect adversely both the writer of long fiction and the writer of short fiction. But the writer of short fiction, if he has read even a little critical comment in an endeavor to inform himself of the essential nature of his art, will have been confused and misdirected by the eternal quarrel over the short story, what it is, whether it is a distinct literary form, its totality or unity of effect, and so forth. I have said much on this head in discussing the short story, and shall not repeat the argument here. It is enough to say that the short story most certainly is a distinct literary form, in that it is brief enough to be read at one sitting and embodies a plot or dramatic problem, which is not true of the tale. But its distinction from other forms of fiction, plotted and unplotted alike, does not lie in its totality or unity of effect, except in the case of the short story of atmosphere. The dramatic short story, whether it stresses character or the event, differs from the novel or romance not in that it possesses a plot —so do the longer types—but in that it is brief. And it differs from the tale—which also is brief—in that it possesses a plot. The short story of atmosphere is abnormal, and a type in itself.

As was stated in the chapter on the short story, the only sense in which the dramatic short story can be said to possess unity is purely verbal. As a mere sequence of words, it possesses unity in that each word is essential to the story. That is not to say that the matter of the story, its people, situations, and settings, is "unified," whatever the word may mean so applied. The form is verbally coherent, but not necessarily coherent in substance, except that it embodies one plot—or story-idea, no more, no less. The one story-idea may involve great diversity in its three elements of people, events, and setting. It would not be worth while to discuss the general false emphasis upon the unity of the short story were it not for the strong tendency of such discussion to lead the writer to devise stories too simple really to interest, apart from the appeal to their characters.

It seems to me that the question of realism and the question of the dramatic short story's assumed unity of substance are the two pitfalls into which the feet of the writer of fiction who reads the mass of comment on his art are most apt to stray. It is difficult enough to find an interesting story without having one eye blinded by a false artistic philosophy. Generally, in reading critical comment on specific stories and authors and on the art of fiction, the writer of fiction will do well to remember that such matter is written for the general reader, not for the practitioner of the art, and that the poor critic must say something! He cannot discuss technique, for he would be both dull and unintelligible to the general reader. So he says what he does.

It remains to state a true artistic philosophy for the writer of fiction, that philosophy which is implied in the content and aim of the art of fiction itself. The content of fiction is man and what he possibly or conceivably may experience; the aim of fiction is to interest. It would be more accurate to state that the content of fiction is personality and what it may experience— witness any animal story, or Kipling's story of a steamship, cited above—but fiction deals so exclusively with man that the first statement may stand.

Since the content of fiction is man and what he possibly or conceivably may experience, the writer of fiction is at liberty to go to fairyland or South Boston, to heaven, hell, or the stock-exchange, for the material for his story. He is subject to no limitations, for whatever he can conceive is open to his use. If he does choose to leave the homely earth, however, he cannot return until he has finished the story. If his story moves in a fairy world subject only to physical laws of its own, such basic conditions of the story must continue to operate. But that is a matter of achieving the aim to interest rather than a matter of content, of telling the story so that it will seem real even though it is unbelievable.

The reader will note that the content of fiction gives him opportunity to write so terrifically "realistic" a thing as Dostoievsky's "House of the Dead," so nobly "romantic" a thing as Hawthorne's "Scarlet Letter," or so finely fantastic a thing as Carroll's "Alice in Wonderland." The sole limitation upon his work is his own conceptive and executive power, unless he foolishly subjects himself to the bondage of some special school. As time goes on, his own essential bent of mind and heart will gradually reveal to him the sort of matter he can handle best.

The influence upon the fiction writer's philosophy of the aim and necessity to interest may now be discussed.

An important point is that there are degrees of interest. A strongly novel course of events will catch and hold a reader's interest, but the interest aroused by a fiction presenting a novel course of events and nothing else is not quite the same thing as the interest aroused by a story which shows real men and women meeting the real problems of life, material or spiritual. The interest aroused by mere novelty is a matter largely of the intelligence; it tends to be evanescent because it has little or no relation to the emotional nature. On the other hand, the other sort of interest, that aroused by the spectacle of real men and women meeting the real problems of life, is deepened and intensified by the emotional element of sympathy and hate for lovable and hateful people. And the real, though perhaps intrinsically simple problems of life—to make a living, win love, overcome temptation—are precisely the problems which are humanly significant because universally experienced. The story which shows real people struggling with such a problem will have a keener interest for a reader through his familiarity with its matter in personal experience. Such a story appeals to the emotions both through its people and through its theme.

This matter is well worth dwelling upon, for, apart from merit in point of executive artistry, the only standard whereby a story can be estimated as relatively significant or relatively insignificant is the standard of interest, that is, interest for the ideal reader, the reader of open and able mind and sympathetic heart. The aim of fiction is to interest, and the story which most deeply interests most completely fulfils the ideals of the art. "Les Miserables" is a greater book than any one of Jules Verne's mechanical romances, not because it is better written, and not because it is a terrific indictment of society—as a modern reviewer might put it—but simply because its people and matter generally arouse the most poignant emotional and intellectual interest in a reader qualified to feel its power. The interest aroused by Verne's sort of story—H. G. Wells' earlier work and Conan Doyle's "The Lost World" are more recent examples—is real, but almost exclusively intellectual, therefore relatively weak and evanescent. Books such as "Les Miserables" cannot be forgotten; the details of the story may vanish from the mind with time; but a reader will retain through life the memory of the book's power, the memory of the eagerness with which he followed the fortunes of its people.

Between masterpieces that will incorporate their essence and memory with a reader's very life—books such as "Les Miserables" and "The Scarlet Letter," to name together the utterly dissimilar—and stories that can serve only to while away an idle hour or two, there are fictions of every sort and condition, the product of all sorts of aims and philosophies, artistic and moral. Apart from the matter of executive artistry, each must take rank as relatively good or relatively feeble in accordance with its power to evoke interest. Some—as the detective story or any story of ratiocination—have in high degree the power to call forth a reader's intellectual interest; some—as the fictional comedy of manners—may interest slightly the mind through their plot and the heart through their people; but each is significant as a fiction solely by virtue of its power to enthrall a reader of open mind and sympathetic heart.

If the power to interest the ideal reader is the sole test of a story's merit as a fiction—and no other test can withstand examination even for a moment—it inevitably follows that to be a masterpiece a story, long or short, must show fictionally real men and women coping with the material and spiritual problems of our common human destiny. No other matter can arouse the deepest and most abiding interest in a reader. However perfect a writer's technique, if he chooses to write of physical or spiritual matters that are relatively trivial and insignificant, he cannot hope to do the finest work. Of course, it is unnecessary to say that the writer of fiction rests under no moral or artistic obligation to attempt a masterpiece in each story he undertakes. He is under obligation to attempt to interest in some degree.

Thus far, in discussing the influence upon the fiction writer's philosophy of the aim and necessity that fiction interest, emphasis has been laid upon the question of matter. But from the aim and necessity results the whole executive technique.

The general proposition is that significant matter cannot arouse a reader's deepest interest unless it is presented to him effectively, nor can relatively insignificant matter arouse whatever interest is attainable by it unless it also is presented effectively. The writer of a story must seek to invest it with reality in the eyes of a reader, and his resources to perform this difficult task make up the body of the technique of fiction.

It follows that the best story in point of executive artistry is the story which realizes most fully the inherent capacity of its matter to interest. However significant the content of a story, if the writer's hand falter in execution, something of the fiction's appeal for a reader will be lost.

The general aim of executive artistry or technique is to invest the story with such reality that a reader will himself see so much of the thing as is physical and feel so much of it as is emotional or spiritual, for only thus can be evoked the full measure of interest inherent in the matter. Unless the writer's words constitute in themselves a primary spectacle and experience for a reader, instead of a mere secondary relation, the story cannot have full effect. A reader will not accept the mere say-so of the writer, who must spread upon his page the very stuff of life itself, rather than mere words.

How difficult the task, it is unnecessary to dwell upon, but one thing should be noted. This necessary power to precipitate reality, this literary power, only infrequently involves writing in a "literary" manner or style. The essence of literary power is to present the particular matter fittingly, not artificially. If the particular story concerns simple, everyday people and simple, everyday events, it should be told in simple, everyday language, for such language will serve best to precipitate the matter for a reader. Literary power is the power to adapt the word to the matter, not the power of "fine" writing. Some stories call for little verbal elaboration, while such a thing as "The Fall of the House of Usher" exhausts the capacities of language, but whatever the nature of any story, its writer's artistry and technical capacity are measurable by the degree in which he succeeds in endowing it with reality and verisimilitude, not by the verbal noise and agility he makes and displays.

Verisimilitude, of course, is a relative term. The matter of the story of everyday life is essentially tangible and concrete, and its writer can invest it with tangibility and concreteness in a degree higher than is attainable by the writer who deals with fantasies and dreams. The measure of verisimilitude attainable by any story is limited by its content. If it deals with fine-spun fancies, it cannot attain the hearty solidity of the story that deals with the matter of fact. No writer can do more than precipitate his conception in his words; if the conception itself is essentially airy and impalpable, so must the story be airy and impalpable. In fact, the perfect fictional illusion is that which most nearly produces on a reader the exact impression the matter would produce if actually experienced. If a story is strictly unbelievable—of course any story is conceivable, or it would not have been written—the writer can do no more than create an illusion of fictional verity, not of literal verity. That is, a reader will accept the author's basic assumptions and the whole story as well, if it is developed logically from the assumptions. Any fairy tale is an instance of what is meant.

I will mention briefly one other consequence of the aim and necessity that fiction interest. Usually the story, or fiction embodying a plot, will interest more deeply than the mere tale. Therefore the writer of fiction usually will choose to write stories rather than tales. The bare fact is that the highest type of fiction, the fiction of greatest power over a reader through its human significance, is adequately plotted simply because it does show real people meeting a real problem of life.

At this point becomes apparent how much that grossly abused word "plot" stands for. Broadly, a plot is a dramatic problem, and a dramatic problem results from the opposition of man and man, the opposition of man and nature, or conflict within a single man. The element of mere complication is not essential to a plot, not being essential to a dramatic problem. "Dramatic situation" is perhaps a better term than "plot," for it has none of the associations of complication that cling to the latter. Even "dramatic situation" is objectionable, because it has connotations of the stage, and suggests an acuteness and tensity, a general brevity and pitch of struggle that is not essential to fiction. "Robinson Crusoe," for instance, though not very tense, is adequately plotted; it shows man's struggle for bread, shelter, and raiment. "Don Quixote" is adequately plotted; it shows man in the grip of a dream, and so at odds with all the world.[U] As stated, all great fiction is adequately plotted simply because it shows real people faced by the real problems of life. The plot of a story of worth stands for its author's effort to isolate one of life's significant elements or problems, and, by showing it in high relief, to invest it with that certain dignity and momentousness, as of life raised to a high power, whereby a reader may be laid under a spell more absolute than any to which the confused and shifting spectacle of life itself can subject him. In the last analysis, great fiction does more than to interest; it whispers to a reader of the significance and worth of human life, and heartens him to live his own.

APPENDIX A

SUGGESTIONS FOR THE STUDENT

It is surely obvious that the only way to learn how to write is—to write. The only way to learn how to do anything is to try until the secret is conquered, and the more difficult the feat or art the longer must be the apprenticeship.

Stepping from abstract study of technique to the actual writing of a story is a violent transition. The student has only a very general knowledge, and now he must give it narrowly specific application. He has read a brief discussion of the mechanics of the art of describing a person, for instance, has read Stevenson's description of Villon and his fellows; now he himself must write a description of Napoleon or Lizzie Smith or John Arthur McAllister; and he desires to write as well as Stevenson.

The only thing to do is to go at the task patiently and with courage. Put the best of you at the moment into each thing you undertake, but do not expect each single item of your work to show an appreciable advance, and do not be discouraged if each thing you do seems as poor or no better than what has gone before. Your first, second, tenth, or fifteenth story may be patent trash, in point of execution, but never mind. After a year or so of intelligent and directed writing the results of your study and application of technique will begin to appear. It is impossible that they should show themselves at once, for technical study will cramp and constrain you until you have gained some real facility in writing in accordance with the canons of art. That is true of all arts, of course. No tool can be used properly without practice.

Perhaps you may desire to submit your practice work to magazines and publishers as you go along, and if you mean to have a serious try at the game it is advisable that you do so. The fact that you are writing for submission will serve as a stimulus; you will receive helpful incidental criticisms from editors, if your work shows promise; and, above all, you will gradually acquire the necessary knowledge of the market, its needs, tendencies, and desires. However, I do not believe it advisable for one who is trying to learn to write to ape deliberately the tone of particular magazines, with an eye to possible sales. That is a trick of the trade—and permissible enough—but it is no way to learn to write fiction. The skilled hand can direct his efforts so, but the apprentice had better center his efforts upon finding some good story and upon writing it to the best he knows how.

A few specific bits of advice as to how to go about practicing the art of fiction may not be useless. Technique is conceptive, constructive, and executive, and the beginner should exercise his latent powers in each department.

The technique of conception is practiced unconsciously by anyone who seeks to find a story for writing, but exercise of the conceptive faculty should not be limited to the times when you desire actually to write. You should form a habit of thinking creatively, of mentally shaping into stories the material offered by observation, thought, and reading. If this is done, and notes kept of your promising ideas, you will have on hand constantly considerable amount of material, and you will not be forced to waste time in casting about for an idea when the spirit moves you to write. Moreover, I think most essentially feeble stories are stories conceived and thrown together on the spur of the moment as the writer sits and looks at a sheet of white paper, and if you have five, ten, or a hundred stories more or less completely blocked out in your files or in your mind, you can choose for writing one fitted to your mood and also worth the writing. It is almost impossible to judge the worth of an idea immediately after it is conceived; by separating the conceptive and executive processes you will be led to avoid much waste labor in developing what is essentially weak.

A more mechanical exercise of the conceptive faculty, but a very valuable one, is to shape and re-shape what I will term abstract stories. As stated, a story or plot is a dramatic conflict, showing the opposition of man and nature, man and man, or opposed traits in the same man. The process of developing an abstract story is to select from a list of human traits and motives two or more which present an essential opposition, such as avarice and generosity, then to seek to give the basic abstract opposition most effective concrete fictional expression by devising persons to be invested with the traits and by devising a course of action to show the persons in conflict under the influence of the traits. Thus, taking the traits of avarice and generosity, husband and wife, for instance, may each be endowed with one, and a course of events devised to give the necessary conflict between them expression in action. The writer of fiction who will perform this exercise now and then, as opportunity offers, not only will chance upon much valuable material; he also will acquire a firm grasp on plot, the story-essence of a story, and will be led to realize that mere complication or ingenuity is the least of a plot. The exercise is valuable because it is the only possible way to exercise the conceptive faculty in detail. A story-idea gained from observation usually is seized as a whole, but a story-idea gained by manipulating human traits and motives is built up from nothing by combining its elements. The story built up in this way probably will involve a social conflict, a conflict between man and man, rather than between man and nature or opposed traits in the same man, because the opportunity for combination is greatest in the first case.

The next point is how to exercise the constructive faculty, how to practice constructive technique, and here you have many resources, only a few of which need be mentioned.

In the first place, you can study the ways the masters have put together their stories; this, though not quite practice, is almost as valuable, if conscientiously and properly done, and is a necessary basis for practice. For obvious reasons your laboratory analysis of fiction must confine itself largely to the short story, though you can go through the process mentally and less thoroughly in reading longer work.

Provide yourself with a collection of short stories in one volume and a few from current magazines that you think good, also with a number of different colored inks or crayons. Read a story through a couple of times, that you may know definitely what it is, and then read it again critically, underlining every word, except those which serve only to forward the progress of the story as a mere course of events, and striking out every word or passage which seems to you inessential to the whole. Use a single color to mark a single process, and neglect the superficial character of the words, whether they be narrative, descriptive, or serve to embody dialogue. Thus, dialogue may serve to forward the progress of the story as a course of events, in which case it should not be underlined, may serve to characterize, in which case it should be underlined with the color taken to mark characterization, or may serve to touch in setting, in which case it should be underlined with the color taken to mark any passage where the author strives to touch in the environment. It will not be profitable to be too minute, to employ too many colors; the matters you will require to make visually distinctive are not many. Straight narration, including the whole physical progress of the story, whether detailed or general, requires no color; characterization, including the process of individualizing a person as to his nature, as to his appearance, and as to his speech, requires one; the process of touching in setting requires another; the process of preparing a reader emotionally for succeeding events requires a third; the process of intensifying atmosphere—if the story is of atmosphere—requires a fourth. And mark each passage in accordance with its main purpose or function, for many passages will subserve more than one end.

A number of stories treated in this way will be most profitable to study. In particular, each one will display graphically and yet in detail wherein lies its value as a fiction, whether in its people, in its events, or in its setting, and will show plainly the cunning blending of elements which is at once the fact and the result of the technique of construction.

In the second place, you can exercise your faculty of construction by closing the decorated book or magazine and trying to reproduce two or three of the stories you have studied. In doing this no effort should be made to transcribe from memory; realize, rather, the basic theme of each story, the general character of its people, and the main course of its events, and strive to produce as effective a thing from such materials as did the author. The very great value of this sort of practice work lies in the fact that you have a positive standard of comparison ready for your story when it is written. Place yours and the original side by side, and you can see precisely where you have failed, if you feel that you have. In examining your own work, look to the matter of expression less than to the matter of construction; see if you have realized the necessity to build character here, to touch in setting there, even if your attempt to do so has failed in a degree through lack of executive deftness.

In the third place, the faculty of construction can be exercised in original work, and to do so does not necessarily involve writing a complete story. Ten stories can be blocked out and roughly shaped in the time it would take to write one, and the more rapid process is preferable for the beginner because it will teach him that the first conception is not usually the best conception. Write thousand-word outlines of ten stories as you have opportunity, put them aside for a while, and then see if you cannot re-shape their people, re-devise and re-order their events, to make them more effective, more interesting fictions. In blocking out a story do not state happenings merely; indicate your people's natures, their looks, their speech, and indicate where you would touch in setting, depict character by action, speech, or description, or hint to a reader the emotional quality of what is to come.

It will take a very real degree of courage and perseverance to carry out a course of practice in conceptive and constructive technique long enough to accomplish its end. But if you will lay out for yourself along the lines indicated here such a course of study and practice, and then will perform the necessary work, you will certainly gain more insight into the essential processes of fiction than you can acquire merely by accepting at face value such story-ideas as may come to you and by writing them out one after the other. In particular, you will acquire the faculty to re-mould and re-shape your material, instead of seizing each idea too uncritically. And that is half the battle, for it is precisely the attitude and habit of the professional as contrasted with the attitude and habit of the amateur.

Little need be said as to the best way to practice the technique of execution. When you find or devise a story that you feel is truly worth the writing, write it as best you can, after careful and directed planning. You can also try to reproduce the work of others, and again the great value of this sort of practice lies in your having a positive standard of comparison ready for your

APPENDIX A - 163

work when it is written. Or you can practice piecemeal, if you have the necessary enthusiasm, can go about with a notebook in your pocket, as did Stevenson, and try to precipitate in telling words the casual impressions that come to you. At all events, write from a primary spectacle, whether of the imagination or of actuality, and try to reproduce something definite in your words rather than to string together vociferous but meaningless phrases.

APPENDIX B

SUGGESTIONS FOR TEACHERS

The instructor in fiction technique has my hearty sympathy. His must be all the woes of manuscript reader, editor, and friend of the author rolled into one.

It would serve no purpose to list here the inherent difficulties of the business of teaching the art of the story, such as that made by the fact that the instructor must deal with a number of individuals differing not only in point of powers but in point of earnestness. But there is reason to note one thing. The aim of the course should not be academic. It should not be allowed to degenerate into a course in the appreciation of fiction, the most constant danger to which lecturing and abstract discussion on fiction technique is subject. The student should not be permitted for a moment, even, to become merely the appraising connoisseur rather than the humble practitioner of the art. Such shifting of viewpoint is fatal.

History can be taught piecemeal; so can mathematics and a hundred other subjects; but the art of fiction cannot, even if it is teachable at all. The one great secret of the art of fiction is the art of construction, and it will profit a class little to assign short exercises in handling specific elements of a story, the elements of personality, event, or setting. The whole secret of fiction writing is to blend all these matters into an interesting and significant whole, and the only way to seek or impart it is to construct and write or to require the class to construct and write whole stories. And the proper use of a text-book, aside from general study by the class and the discussion of reading-assignments, is for reference in criticising the stories that have been written by and read before the class.

The general aim of the teacher should be to keep the student writing, but writing with a definite aim. The simplest sort of story to write, of course, is the story of plain action, and, concomitantly with discussion of plot, it will be advisable to outline for writing two or three relatively simple stories. Choose these from magazines not too recent; give the class the main course of events, the people, and the setting to work from; and read the original story when reading and discussing the work of the class, for a fixed standard of comparison is extremely valuable. As the course proceeds, more complicated stories can be outlined for reproduction, and from the first it will be useful to require the student to hand in with the story he has written an outline of a story of the same general type, but original with himself. After telling the class where they may find each story they have unconsciously worked upon, state its chief values as succinctly as possible, and point out wherein each student's work has or has not realized such values, and also indicate any value in the class-work not present in the original. Incidentally, point out the merits and defects of the original outlines handed in with the complete stories. Of course, the whole business must be highly selective; discuss fully a little of the best work, rather than say a few inadequate words as to each student's.

As the opportunity offers, it will be advisable to engage in oral story-building with the class. State two or more traits or motives that involve a conflict, and then call upon individuals to outline a story presenting the dramatic opposition. Or assign for reading a particular newspaper of particular date, and require individuals first to state what news item seems to offer the best suggestion for a story and then to outline the story suggested by it. This sort of work is extremely valuable in itself and to keep the class from forgetting that they are trying to learn the secret to find, develop, and write good stories.

Finally, as to the matter of original work. When the student is asked completely to develop and write a story of his own, it will be best to let him work in any direction he pleases, rather than to require him to show some particular type of story. The matter of type can be touched on in discussion. And, to emphasize the importance of construction, it will be well to require submission of a completely developed outline of each story before writing, also to discuss and re-shape these with the class, stating their outstanding values and weaknesses. The general endeavor should be to impress upon each student the fact that the material of fiction is infinitely plastic, so that he should shape and re-shape his conception before writing until he is certain that he has exhausted its possibilities. The matter of verbal execution should not be given any great emphasis simply because it cannot be treated in class with any great profit. The instructor can say that this passage is bad and that good, hardly more. But a poorly constructed story can be taken apart and rearranged more effectively, and the process can be grasped by the student because it is somewhat mechanical. Furthermore, the technique of fiction and the technique of verbal expression are different matters, and the instructor in the first will be wise if he leaves the matter of nice expression to the instructor in the second. Of course, obvious verbal crudities in class work should be pointed out.

The real service that a course in technique can perform for an earnest student is threefold. It can lead him to realize keenly that the aim of fiction is to interest, that this aim can be attained most completely by presentment of a human conflict or problem, and that adequate fictional presentment of such a conflict, problem, or plot is to be achieved only by a cunning blending of the elements of personality, event, and setting. That course in fiction technique is the best course which does the most to open the eyes of the student to the essential nature of the art and most definitely shows him the matters he must bear in mind in putting together a story. If he leaves the hands of the instructor with a knowledge of the fundamentals of construction, the instructor will have done well.

APPENDIX C

TO WRITE A STORY

CONCEPTIVE TECHNIQUE

(1) Find your story, a fiction exhibiting personality in conflict with its environment, with another personality, or with itself.

(2) Realize precisely what constitutes the plot—what opposition between what forces of personality or nature is the influence which gives fictional significance to the sequence of incidents or events that have first come to mind as the story.

(3) Realize the characters, major and minor; that is, discover just what attributes of theirs must be developed by direct statement or by inference from action in order to give the plot an adequate, concrete, specific presentment.

(4) Having grasped the plot, the essence of the story, and all its implications, and having realized the individual people who alone can present it convincingly, scrutinize closely the events of the story, as they first were conceived, to discover whether their rearrangement or entire change may not result in a combination presenting the plot more adequately and more forcefully than the combination that first suggested the plot.

(5) Having blocked out the fiction thus, consider and determine from whose viewpoint it may best be told.

CONSTRUCTIVE TECHNIQUE

(1) Arrange the significant events of the story in sequence with a due but not forced regard to the necessities of climax, that is, increasing tensity of the plot-struggle.

(2) Consider how best to link together the major happenings, and endeavor to devise and manipulate the minor events so that they may serve a double purpose, first, to lead from major event to major event, second, to develop the characters; remember that a story is a physical presentment of a spiritual thing, the plot-struggle, and that personality should function in

the small as well as in the great events.

(3) Determine precisely the ending toward which to work, and let it coincide with the termination of the plot-struggle.

(4) Apportion the length of the story among its several happenings, those main events which give physical presentment to the plot and so incidentally develop or exhibit character, and those minor events which only develop character or merely aid the physical progress of the story.

EXECUTIVE TECHNIQUE

(1) Determine the style or manner of writing for which the story calls, and maintain it when once pitched upon.

(2) Write vividly only where emphasis is called for by the event; do not be afraid to narrate in general terms where the story does not call for detail; and think less of the word than of the thing you visualize. Let the story flow before your eye and sound in your ear as to an actual observer or listener; transcribe only what he would see, hear, smell or think under the influence of the particular circumstances.

(3) Avoid all artificialities, in description, in the speech of characters, even in their names and in the undue repetition of verbs of utterance—"he said," "she said."

(4) Re-write, or touch up in manuscript.

(5) After a week or more, when other matters have shaken the mind from the ruts it has worn for itself in planning and writing the story, re-read it critically to discover whether it is worth-while and whether it cannot be improved.

FOOTNOTES:

[A] One might expand here on the distinction that in the story stressing character it is the particular persons who interest the reader, while in the story of plot his interest centers in the events, and the people of the story are followed less as individuals than as the human focal points whereon the events take effect. Such fine analysis is tempting, but of little use, for any story is a compact unity of the three elements.

[B] Polti, in "The Thirty-Six Dramatic Situations," uses the word "situation" in a sense practically inclusive of plot. Plot is a word so abused that it even might be advisable to abandon it in discussion in favor of situation. The latter suggests more nearly the requisite idea of persons keyed for struggle. In particular, plot carries too many connotations of mere complication, which is not one of its essential qualities.

[C] In discussing the principles of construction it is obviously impossible to illustrate the text by quotation, for just construction could be shown only by reprinting an entire story. The reader must supplement what is said here by independent analytical reading. The only fortunate thing about the situation is that the matters which can be adequately illustrated by brief quotations—such as vividness in narrating—are chiefly matters of execution and least subject to profitable objective study.

[D] This story is a particularly instructive instance of how much the secondary events are within the writer's control, and also of how much depends on their just selection and ordering. The twin plot themes of the book are the struggle of man with man and the struggle of man with nature; they are developed almost entirely without aid from the superficially main events of the story, Maud's coming aboard the schooner and what follows. That is precisely the artistic defect of the work.

[E] The three fundamental plot themes are man's struggle with nature, man's struggle with man, and man's struggle with himself. The human element is inherently a part of any plot.

[F] It would be difficult to overstate how much of its appeal such a story as Fannie Hurst's "T. B.," reprinted in "The Best Short Stories of 1915," owes to its author's careful development of the personality of Sara Juke. Yet the story is not strictly a character story. In less competent hands the bare story would have been nothing; as it is, it is a fiction of real worth and significance.

[G] I will note here a matter suggested rather than stated by the general discussion, which is intended to be practical rather than philosophical. Narration must be in the first or third person, but the two fundamental types are personal and impersonal narration, and the line between them is not drawn by the pronouns I and he. Truly, when the story is told in the first person, the writer adopts the personal viewpoint of the narrating character, but when the writer chooses to write in the third person he also adopts the personal viewpoint of the character of whose soul he assumes knowledge, if he does so as to the soul of only one. This is the case, with a shifting personal viewpoint, when the writer assumes knowledge of the minds and souls of several characters, but not of all. Assuming knowledge of the soul of a character necessarily involves looking at the world through his eyes. It results that the only real impersonal viewpoint is to write in the third person and either to renounce all knowledge of motives or to assume knowledge of all events and the spirits of all the characters, when the reader will gain the impression of an impersonal relator rather than of a shifting personal viewpoint. The point is of no great importance, but realization of it may be of some slight service. In particular, if the story is told in the third person, but from the viewpoint of a single major character, universal knowledge of events cannot be assumed.

[H] The writer should strive to realize this fact. The necessity is not to make the reader accept a story as literal truth, but to make him accept it as fictional truth. Many of Poe's stories are unbelievable, but their power is felt to the full though they are not believed. In other words, the reader will grant the author his premises.

[I] In connection with the subject of vivid narration of an important event I might illustrate the text by brief quotation. Unlike matters of construction, matters of strict execution can be shown by pungent quotation. The question is not whether it is possible, but whether it is useful. Take this sentence from Stevenson's "Kidnapped": "His sword flashed like quicksilver into the huddle of his fleeing enemies." It is perfectly descriptive, alive as the sword was alive in the hand of Alan Breck. But no one by reading it can learn to write like it, a capacity to be gained only by long and arduous practice, such as Stevenson's. A good many books on technique have more quotation than text, and while free quotation lends a superficial weight to the whole, it is not of much practical use to one seeking to learn how to write. His own reading will offer him examples in plenty, and the most or even the only useful thing a work on technique can do for him is to state the principles he should try to follow in his own work.

[J] I once read a story in manuscript wherein a character related a commonplace tale of woe to another, with the result that the other's eyes "glistened with hot tears." Not only has the expression been worked to death, so that it has no primary freshness for a reader, but it is too artificial and strained for a story of the commonplace.

[K] A good deal of abstract statement might be made as to the description of persons, but the main considerations have been stated. The whole philosophy of this phase of technique rests on the necessity that every line of a story be given as much as possible of the concreteness and vivacity of life. It is useless to give a long description of a character once and for all when he first comes up in a story. Even if a reader gains a sharp impression therefrom, he will not carry it with him through the succeeding events involving the character. His first impression of the person must be kept alive by repeated descriptive touches, not so much because the person must be described adequately as because every part of the story must have the body of life. The distinction is fine, but real, and perhaps may be made clearer by imagining a reader witnessing an event in which a friend is involved. He knows his friend, as he can know no character in a story; nevertheless he sees him uninterruptedly as the event develops. To counterfeit the process in a story, descriptive touches as to the persons must be interspersed with the narrative matter, though the persons have been described already. A story should describe persons in action and repose.

[L] The writer should not have an eye to the origin of his words only while writing dialogue. In narrating the homely and commonplace event, and in describing everyday scenes, where the value lies in everyday associations, the suggestive English word should be used. The matter has been touched upon, though not in these terms. The whole endeavor in fiction writing generally should be to make the word chime with the substance.

[M] A great deal of close argument might be developed here. A plot is a chain of events influencing and influenced by character, and by character is meant not persons but traits. In some story, let us say, the avarice of one man brings him into conflict with another, also impelled by avarice. The conflict, of course, is not between two disembodied attributes, but between two persons, and the writer of such a story must individualize them. He should endeavor to give a reader an idea of how they look, by describing them, and of how they talk, by individualizing their speech. But he need not emphasize nor even bring out any phase of their spiritual natures not material to the story. That is to say, the writer of a story, in order to give it the seeming of life, should make every effort and employ all means to invest each character with a definite physical presence or illusion of actuality, but he should not try to displace the inner nature of each person in like detail.

[N] It will be instructive to realize why direct statement of a character's outstanding moral quality is less effective than skillful description of his person, though both the statement and the description are fundamentally descriptive writing. One may say that a moral attribute cannot be described, can merely be stated, but that is a statement of the condition rather than of the cause. The root of the matter is that the appearance of a person is the resultant of a combination of details; by stating the significant details in proper relation the writer can force a reader to perceive for himself the totality of the person's appearance. But a quality of soul is unified and undetailed. It is ineffective to say that a person is cruel simply for the same reason that it is ineffective to say that he is handsome. It follows that any breaking up of a quality of soul into its elements, if possible, will increase the effectiveness of the statement. Thus, cruelty may result from essential virility of soul in combination with insensitiveness, and so forth.

[O] To accomplish this subordinate and strictly unnecessary characterization the writer must employ the same three means of speech, direct statement, and action. But the action will constitute only a secondary event or events in the story, and must not bulk too large at the expense of the primary events.

[P] Of course, the initial conception of a story of atmosphere may limit the writer's power to manipulate his material. Thus when Stevenson pitched upon the emotional effect of the west coast of Scotland as that to be produced by "The Merry Men," he debarred himself from placing his story in any other setting, though he could pick and choose freely among possible events and people. A general emotional effect, as of beauty, is somewhat indefinite, and may be produced alike by stories differing widely in their three elements of setting, people and events.

[Q] The root cause of all the unintelligent discussion of the short story's unity in books on technique is failure to distinguish between form and content. The mere fact that no word without relation to the story-idea can be transcribed does not mean that the story-idea—complex of people, events, and settings—is a unity. The short story is a unit in that it is one story, rather than two or ten, but—it is not impertinent to ask—what of it? A single story may involve great diversity and complication of elements. And it is what is known as a short story if it can be presented adequately within some few thousand words, though it begin in a king's palace with tragedy and end in laughter in a Harlem flat. Poe's type of short story is another matter; it does possess unity of content in that setting, personality, and events are subtly alike.

[R] For a plainer, because less philosophical discussion of the fallacies of realism, the artistic philosophy, see p. 199.

[S] "The Ebb-Tide" is interesting in connection with the general question of plot. Its plot is the struggle within Robert Herrick between an artificially stimulated resolution and an essential weakness of moral fibre. The mere mechanical complication that he and his fellows steal a schooner laden with bottled water thinking her laden with champagne is no part of the plot, only a circumstance of the action, yet, as plot is commonly understood, the circumstance would be taken as the heart of the plot in itself. Also, "The Ebb-Tide" is interesting in connection with the matter of realism and the fallacies of the cult. The realists might claim the book, but they would have a merry time to point any essential difference between it and "The Master of Ballantrae," which they would reject. And a distinction that can be justified only when applied to extreme types-say "Pride and Prejudice" and "Frankenstein"—is not very convincing.

[T] In a sense, the mind is of the body rather than of the soul, where it functions in the common business of life.

[U] Dostoievsky's "The Idiot" should be compared with "Don Quixote," for the fundamental theme of each book is the same.

SERIES BIBLIOGRAPHY

Recommended Books on Writing

Becoming the Fiction Storyteller of Your Dreams
Dorothea Brande, Marie Shedlock, Robert C. Worstell

The Elements of Style
William Strunk, Jr.

Short Story Writing
Charles Raymond Barrett

Fiction Writing Technique
Robert Saunders Dowst

Recommended Books on Illustration

How to Become a Pro Pencil Drawing Artist
Thrive Learning Institute Library

The Elements of Drawing
John Ruskin

The Practice and Science of Drawing
Harold Speed

Pen Drawing – An Illustrated Treatise
Charles Donagh Maginnis & Garrett Putman Serviss

Line and Form
Walter Crane

Crayon Portraiture
Jerone A. Barhydt

Getting Introduced to Oil Painting
Thrive Learning Institute Library

The Painter in Oil: A Complete Treatise
Daniel Burleigh Parkhurst

Recommended Books on Self-Publishing

Just Publish! Ebook Creation for Indie Authors
Robert C. Worstell

RESOURCES

Visit <u>Midwest Journal Press</u> for more material and related books.

http://picturebook.midwestjournalpress.com